Making It As A Makeup Artist:

A Guide to Becoming a Working Freelance Makeup Artist

by
Frida Bell

Copyright © 2016 by Frida Bell

All rights reserved. This book or any portion thereof

may not be reproduced or used in any manner whatsoever

without the express written permission of the publisher

except for the use of brief quotations in a book review.

Cover artwork by Stig Kristensen; copyright © 2016.

Printed in the United Kingdom

First Printing, 2016. Updated 2018.

Table of Contents

INTRODUCTION 7

CHAPTER ONE - FIRST STEPS 9
Business Plan 12
Know Your Industry 17
Insurance 19
   Recommendations 22
Registering as Self-Employed 23
Paying Taxes 30
Personal Presentation 34

CHAPTER TWO - GAINING EXPERIENCE 37
Study 37
   Different Types of Courses 40
Work 43
   How to Get a Job at MAC 44
Assist 58
   Tips on Being a Good Assistant 64

CHAPTER THREE - STARTING YOUR KIT 68
Discount Brands 69
Finding Inspiration 75
Kit Tips & Hacks 76
How to Travel With Your Kit 79

CHAPTER FOUR - BUILDING A PORTFOLIO 83
Test Shoots 83
Working For Free – When Tests Aren't Tests At All 89
What Should A Portfolio Contain? 96
Ways to Support Yourself When Building Your
Portfolio 98

CHAPTER FIVE - NETWORKING 100
Weekly Checklist 100
People As Currency 103

CHAPTER SIX - MARKETING YOURSELF 105
Branding 105
Building A Website 108
Business Cards 110
Social Media 111
Editorials / Show Reels 115
Traditional Marketing 117
MLMs 119
Setting Your Rates 120

CHAPTER SEVEN – HOW TO WORK FASHION WEEK
.... 125

CHAPTER EIGHT - PRO DISCOUNTS 129
A-F 129
G-M 136
N-T 142
U-Z 147
Types of Supporting Documents: 148

CHAPTER NINE – HOW TO GET SENT FREE PRODUCTS 151

CHAPTER TEN – MANAGING FINANCES 157
Banking 157
Bookkeeping 158
Chasing Late Payments 162
Late Payment Fees 162
Small Claims Court 164
Report to BECTU 166
Budgeting 166

CHAPTER ELEVEN – GETTING AN AGENT 169
Agent Meetings 173

5

Getting Jobs 175
Final Word 178
About the Author 181

INTRODUCTION

You've either downloaded this book because you're an aspiring makeup artist or perhaps an existing one looking for some tips & ideas you may not have thought of. There are a multitude of help books for US-based makeup artists but next to none for those of us working in the UK. **The British fashion industry alone generates £59 billion** annually (just one sector a makeup artist could work in) with more and more creative talent flocking to London and other cities each year - it's about time someone wrote a book catering to the rapidly growing makeup artist community here in the United Kingdom!

This book is purely about the business of working as a freelance makeup artist; I won't be getting into the history of makeup, brush techniques, or how to contour – there are plenty of resources out there on these topics already. Instead, I'm going to lift the veil on the all-too-often forgotten about business side of things, and show you exactly how to kick-start your freelance makeup career (and keep it running successfully).

Whether you're a beginner or an already working artist, there will be something in this book to help you take your career to the next level.

So let's get started!

CHAPTER ONE - FIRST STEPS

So you've decided to become a makeup artist - congratulations and welcome to this exciting community! But where does one even start?

There are so many different areas a makeup artist can work in and there's no right or wrong way to craft a successful career in your chosen field. That's both the beauty and the frustrating part about this type of work; go read some interviews with some of the world's top makeup artists about how they got their 'big break' and you'll be reading a million different stories. The reality is, there is no 'one size fits all' path or quick fix shortcut, and you'll need to think outside of the box to get ahead and stand out from the crowd – especially in today's competitive world now more than ever.

So first, let's break it down and summarise some of the different areas a makeup artist can work in:

- Fashion Editorial
- Commercial
- Film & TV
- Theatre
- Bridal
- Retail
- Corporate
- Teaching
- Body/Face Painting
- Private Clients (Lessons; Special Occasions)
- Salons
- Social Media (Blog/YouTube/Instagram tutorials, etc)

Most artists will likely combine several of these areas to support a full-time income, so you won't necessarily be locked into a specific industry. In fact, the more you can diversify your portfolio and skills, the more money you will make as you'll have more to offer clients. For example, you may focus in the film industry by doing special effects but also do body or face painting at events on the side. Or you could be an artist working in editorial and commercial fashion, but have developed good enough hair skills to work with bridal clients, too.

But it's also good to have a general idea of what direction you'd like to take your career in when initially starting out, because you will need to focus on some kind of niche. If your portfolio of work is all over the place – corporate headshots next to tear sheets from Vogue and photos of face painting from that last kid's party you did – clients won't know what to hire you for.

If you've been doing some research already on how to get started, you've undoubtedly heard the term, "freelance makeup artist". Freelance simply means you are self-employed and your business is mobile in nature, i.e. you will be travelling around between different clients and workplaces for the jobs that you get booked on. There's also the option to join existing companies as a more traditional, hired employee while working as an artist (we'll go over this more in "Chapter Two – Gaining Experience").

So when visualising how you'd like to work as a makeup artist and how you want your career to look, start by deciding whether you'd like to become freelance or to find a company you can work for – or a mix of both! Think about what works for you and what your ideal career would look like.

Business Plan

Once you have an idea of the path you'd like to take as an artist, realise that as of today you are now your own business. I firmly believe that every single business, no matter the industry, needs a clearly outlined business plan to succeed; this sounds obvious but for some reason many makeup artists I encounter never even consider making a business plan; perhaps because it's "just makeup" and often seen as a somewhat less formal industry (or worse, that it's just a hobby). But make no mistake, you will be getting paid for your services - this is a business. And you need to treat it as such, otherwise you risk floundering or stagnating while others succeed.

So now that you've thought about the general idea of what area(s) you'd like to specialise in, my advice would be to sit down at your computer, fire up Word, and physically compose your business plan. Include things like:

- What kind of artist do you want to be?
- What market will you be working in? i.e. London, Manchester, or maybe a countryside location that's popular for weddings, etc.
- Who are your clients?
- What is your USP (Unique Selling Point)?
- First year business goals
- Artist(s) whose work/career you aspire to

Example:

"I want to be a freelance makeup artist working in the fashion editorial and commercial industries in London, with a specialisation in body painting and creative, avant garde makeup, similar to Isamaya Ffrench. My clients will be both high-end fashion publications and commercial fashion clients and production companies.

I will achieve this by first studying on a body painting course, then assisting established artists while I build my own portfolio and roster of clients of my own.

My first year goals are to have at least ten new portfolio pictures, three regular clients, and earn £2,000 gross profit."

The plan can be amended as your business grows so don't worry if it's not completely perfect right away. You don't have to go out and read a ton of books about crafting the most academically correct business plan ever – as long as it makes sense to *you*. You don't even have to show it to anyone else. The aim is simply for you to have a clear idea of who you want to be, your USP, and where you will fit into this already crowded industry. This will really help you with marketing and how you present yourself to potential clients down the line.

If you really aren't sure about your goals yet, it may help to take some time exploring different areas of makeup artistry first, e.g. studying a makeup course or working on a beauty counter. This can really help you to discover where your strengths and weaknesses lie. Getting real world experience like this is invaluable and you might surprise yourself with what you discover. For example, when I first started out, I undertook a course that primarily focused on special effects makeup for film and television but by the end of it I had shifted my interests entirely to fashion makeup and have stuck on that route ever since. I also tried working retail artist jobs early on in my career, but I found my temperament just didn't suit that environment at all. So I simply adjusted my goals and reworked my business plan a little once I knew better what worked for me (and what didn't).

So whenever you have your first drafted business plan complete, save it to a new folder on your computer or where ever you'd like to store all your important makeup-related documents. This will be a document you can hold yourself accountable against, so to speak, and refer to every now and then if you feel yourself losing direction or filled with self-doubt (which I promise you, will happen many times throughout your career). I like to adjust my plan annually and then reference it again at the end of every year to chart my progress and make any adjustments for the upcoming year. If you do this, you'll always be striving for improvement and this will help you naturally progress to the next level, rather than stagnate.

I know it sounds like I'm asking you to over-think this, when a makeup career should be about fun and creativity, right? But I promise you this will help you so much down the line; it's something I never gave a second thought to when starting out (and was never taught by my expensive makeup school) but having a clear business plan has been a huge determining factor in taking my career from 'newbie MUA' to 'actually making a living at this makeup stuff'.

Know Your Industry

It's important when entering any industry to know the key players within it. No one else can do this part for you so spend as much time as you can researching who the top photographers are, the models, the magazines, designers, competing makeup artists, hair stylists, stylists, film directors, wedding planners, job board websites… anything and anyone you can think of pertaining to your chosen field. This will help you navigate your chosen field so much easier and will give you a leg up on jobs if you get a client who makes an industry specific reference (e.g. "We want something really OTT on the eyes, think Pat McGrath couture runway!")

What's a great, fun resource for this to get started? YouTube! Watch old runway shows, interviews with industry professionals, and documentaries about the greats of your field. Or start up a subscription to Vogue to start learning the names currently in fashion and discover what each designer's aesthetic is - or simply Google what you want to know. We live in an age where you have all the free knowledge in the world available at the click of a mouse – don't take this for granted.

If you're going into bridal artistry, it's a good idea to get an overall scope of the bridal scene in your area so you could start by finding out who runs the top wedding blogs in the UK, what kind of content gets posted there, plus check out your local wedding vendors (venues, wedding planners, dressmakers, etc). Or contact an artist who purely specialises in bridal work to see if you could assist them on one of their upcoming jobs. There are also bridal teams you can join, like an agency, so see if there are any of these in your area, too.

No one's going to give you a pop quiz on this stuff but it's never a bad idea to educate yourself as much as possible on your chosen industry. It'll at the very least help you feel less like a rookie while you're just starting out and give you some inspiration for your own career.

Insurance

I've met a shocking number of makeup artists who don't have insurance. Yes, you read that right – they work every day on people's skin, putting both their clients' health at risk and themselves at risk to be sued for so many unforeseen accidents and they *don't* have insurance.

As soon as you begin working as a freelance makeup artist, purchasing insurance needs to be at the top of your 'to do' list. It's not required by law to have insurance, but I can't think of a single reason why you wouldn't want to protect yourself with a policy. If you've been holding off on sorting it out, the benefits of being covered are endless – help with or total cover of legal costs, protecting against kit theft/loss, covering medical bills of clients who experience adverse reactions... the peace of mind knowing you're covered is alone worth the cost. Plus, many jobs will require you're insured and ask for proof of it, too.

There are many different types of insurance for freelance artists and it can be confusing to understand all the terms the companies may use. Generally speaking, the types of cover you'll want to be included in your policy are things like:

- **Public Liability Insurance**
  This protects you from the costs of legal fees stemming from claims if a member of the public is injured by you, or by any accidents that may occur when you are carrying out your job. It will also cover you if

you damage property belonging to someone else while carrying out business activities.

- **Professional Indemnity Insurance**
Provides cover for legal costs and expenses in defending a claim against a client who has alleged you provided them an inadequate service. It also covers any compensation you may have to pay your client to rectify your error if found liable.

- **Product Liability Insurance**
This usually covers a specified amount of damages you may be awarded should your kit or its contents be damaged in any way or even in the case of theft.

It's boring but you really do need to read the small print for each and every policy you're looking at to make sure it covers both the type of work you do (mobile makeup artistry) and anything you could potentially be sued for or need to claim for. If you can't get your head around the terms, find a friend or family member who has a brain for this kind of stuff to help you go through it, or there are also lots of online forums that will have the information you need.

You run the risk of seriously damaging someone's health – or worse – without proper insurance, so please do not take that chance of working without it just to skimp on a bit of money. Your insurance policy could very well protect you against having your business go under should a claim be made against you.

Recommendations

- BECTU - *www.bectu.org.uk*
- BABTAC - *www.babtac.com*
- Salon Gold - *www.salongold.co.uk*
- NASMAH - *www.nasmah.co.uk*
- Simply Business - *www.simplybusiness.co.uk*

Note: I have no affiliations with any of the above companies and you do not have to purchase policies from any of them; they are listed purely on the basis of being popular choices amongst artists I know and are listed simply as starting off points for you to research thoroughly all available options before selecting the right kind of insurance for you.

Also, I highly recommend you go with a company that specialises in cover for this kind of work (makeup artists, beauty therapists, hairdressers, and so on) as they will be more familiar with the law in case you do have an emergency and need to claim compensation through them. It's just reassuring working with a company who understands all the nuances of our unique field of work.

Registering as Self-Employed

When earning money as a freelance makeup artist, you are required by law to declare all of your income to HMRC (Her Majesty's Revenue & Customs – a.k.a., the tax office). You do this by registering with them as a self-employed 'sole trader' and sending them completed self-assessment tax forms once a year. You can either fill these out yourself online or via post, or hire an accountant to do it for you.

Now, I'm not a tax lawyer and I'm not here to give you tax advice. It's another not-so-fun part of being a makeup artist that you simply have to dedicate some time researching about it on the Internet and educating yourself about how it all works, otherwise you run the risk of getting yourself into some serious legal (and financial) trouble. But I'll try and break it down a little, as it can be so confusing to navigate.

Essentially, the very first step is going to HMRC's website (*www.gov.uk*) to register as self-employed. Navigate yourself to the relevant 'Self-Employed' section, which will guide you through the whole registration process step-by-step. It's very straightforward and easy; they'll just ask you to fill out details about yourself and your new business.

As soon as you are registered, you will need to save every single receipt you get while conducting business and start keeping detailed records of your accounts, if you haven't already. This means tracking your incoming and outgoing business expenses so HMRC knows how much money you're earning and if your earnings are high enough to pay tax. See Chapter Ten on Managing Finances for some tips on how best to keep track of finances.

We keep these detailed records not only because we need to be able to tell HMRC about every single transaction we make as a business, but also because many of the things you will purchase while working are actually tax deductable and this will need to be calculated to determine your annual income. For example, this means if you earn £100 on a job (referred to as your "gross income") but have to spend £25 on relevant business costs, such as travel and equipment, HMRC will only tax you for the remaining £75 (your "net income", i.e. your take home pay).

Examples of items that are tax exempt are for makeup artists:
- Trade magazines (e.g. Vogue)
- Makeup products
- Brushes
- Kit bags and accessories
- Disposables (tissue, cotton pads, etc)
- Travel (there's some small print to read through if you're using your vehicle for personal use also, however, as not everything is deductable)

Really spend a good amount of time educating yourself about what qualifies and what doesn't, because there are a lot of murky areas in regards to what can be claimed as tax deductable and what can't. For example, you cannot claim clothing as an expense unless it has your business logo visible on it to demonstrate it is used solely for work – even you've bought all black clothing that you only use for work, that will not count unless it has your logo on it. The general hard rule to stick by is: if you purchased it and use it purely for your business, it's *likely* it will be deductable… but always check with a qualified tax lawyer/accountant first to be sure. You can run into a lot of trouble if you try to claim things as tax deductable that aren't eligible, as it can look like you're trying to dodge paying tax.

Another tip that you might not know about is that if your annual net income is under a certain amount (for the 2017-18 tax year, it's £11,500 – this amount fluctuates annually so be sure to check each year), it is classified as tax-free income as your earnings are so low – read about "personal allowances" online for full details on this. However, keep in mind you'll need to alert HMRC of your low earnings by applying for something called an "Exemption Certificate from Class 2 National Insurance Contributions". It's a simple, short form you fill out and post to them to inform them of your low earnings, which then will be marked down on your tax record. Once you start earning over the tax-free threshold, however, you must remember to let HMRC know immediately so you can start getting taxed at the regular national rate.

HMRC actually have a really informative YouTube channel with help and tutorial videos aimed at self-employed workers. Their videos help break down all the terminology that can be extremely confusing and off-putting at first. I highly recommend you watch some short clips before completing your first self-assessment form so you get a good idea of all the phrases you'll need to be familiar with and what they will ask of you. You can view the HMRC channel at: *www.youtube.com/user/HMRCgovuk*.

Finally, to organise all this new information you're going to be processing, I'd suggest buying a few cheap A4 expanding folders (the kind that fan out with different sections) and label them:

1. Tax Year 2017-18 (or whatever year you're in)
2. Receipts
3. Other Documents

In the 'Tax Year' folder, keep anything pertaining to tax, i.e. your self-assessment forms for that year, letters from the tax office, tax exemption certificates, and so on. Make a new one each year.

The 'Receipts' folder is self-explanatory. Start putting all your saved receipts in there, preferably sorted by date to make them easier to find when you need them. I also keep all my bank deposit receipts I get when I deposit petty cash, which technically probably isn't really required but I like to write on the back of the slips what job the money was from (e.g. "13 Mar 2016, Actor Headshots, £200"), as you'll sometimes get paid in cash and I like to show a clear record of where each cash deposit came from.

And for 'Other Documents', put anything relating to your business that doesn't fall into the above two categories. This could be any contracts you receive, call sheets you'd like to save, login details, business cards, pro discount cards - whatever. Simply having these three separate folders to organise things as you operate business throughout the year will make your life so much easier come self-assessment form time, I guarantee you.

Paying Taxes

Taxes work much differently when you're self-employed. You'll be in charge of filing your own annual tax return (or you can pay an accountant to do it for you). Because you work for yourself, taxes obviously aren't taken out of a monthly pay check like if you were an employee of a company (i.e. the PAYE system). Instead, you'll have to pay taxes in *advance* based on your income from the previous tax year; which can really bite you in the butt if you had a great year in 2016 but a bad one in 2017 (of course anything you overpay in tax will eventually be refunded but you still must pay upfront and it can often be an unwelcome hit to your business).

Also you don't file and settle the bill for your self-assessment return immediately after one tax year ends, you wait until the next year to file. For example, for the 2016-17 tax year (April 2016 – March 2017), the self-assessment wasn't due until January 31st 2018. Of course you can file earlier, but they won't accept payment of any taxes until January 31st.

Of course, when you're just starting out, your earnings will very likely be under the Personal Allowance threshold (remember the £11,500 mentioned above?) so HMRC won't tax you at all. But the first year you *do* qualify to be taxed, you'll not only have to pay for the previous year's tax in one lump sum, you'll have to pay for the first half of the following year, too! This advance payment is referred to as 'Payments on Account', and is due twice a year, January and July.

So the first year of being taxed really sucks because you're essentially paying for 1.5 years of tax all in one go – which doesn't really seem fair to a small business that's only just finding its feet and becoming profitable, but it's unfortunately the way the system works. It can be really scary and if you weren't prepared for this huge outgoing expense, it can be extremely difficult to manage (luckily if you find yourself in this situation and are really struggling, HMRC has something called a 'Budget Payment Plan' wherein they'll work with you to customise a payment plan to pay the sum over several months instead of all at once).

On top of this, once you earn over £6,025 annually, you'll need to pay Class 2 National Insurance contributions, and if over £8,164 you'll also need to pay Class 4 National Insurance contributions (figures accurate as of December 2017). These amounts will be calculated into HMRC's evaluation of what you need to pay in those twice-annual payments.

There are a lot of variables that will depend on your own personal circumstances so I'd advice either spending a good amount of time researching how all this will affect you or hiring someone to do it for you.

Finally, a good tip now that you're self-employed and earning enough to be taxed, is to open a separate bank account and put 20% of all your earnings in there as soon as you're paid. Don't think of it as being 'your money' – it is technically tax money you'll eventually have to pay and if you have it squirreled away somewhere safe, it won't be such a shock when you do have to pay that first huge tax bill or any subsequent ones. Also, find an account with the highest interest you can; funnily enough, the best rates at the moment can be found on current accounts (Money Saving Expert compares all the top offers at: *www.moneysavingexpert.com/banking/compare-best-bank-accounts*). After all, if you're going to have that money just sitting there, may as well have it working for you and earning you some extra cash while it's waiting to go off to HMRC!

Personal Presentation

So now you're all set up behind the scenes and ready to go out into the workforce! A burning question you may be worrying about before embarking on your first real job is: what should you wear? You want to project a professional image, so it absolutely is an important topic to consider.

Generally speaking, you may have noticed the makeup artist's "unofficial uniform" is an all black outfit. It's very important to remember you'll likely be on your feet and moving around for long hours at a time, so it's vital you wear comfortable shoes (any colour is fine) and free flowing, unrestrictive clothing. Your outfit doesn't have to be office formal, so really any kind of black clothing is fine as long as it's generally workplace appropriate.

Of course there are many artists who wear whatever they want and that's perfectly fine, too. But when just starting out, you're trying to avoid giving anyone the impression that you're an amateur who doesn't know what he or she is doing – wearing an all black, uniform-like ensemble will help you avoid this label as opposed to showing up in blue jeans and a graphic t-shirt. Plus, as you'll quickly learn, black clothing hides makeup smudges so much better!

Keep in mind, however, if you're working for a company, you will need to find out what their uniform policy is and stick to it, as you are representing them as a brand, not your own personal brand. For example, many bridal teams will have their own branded t-shirts you'll be required to wear; this is so it essentially works as free advertising for them in client's wedding photographs.

Also I'd advise against wearing excess jewellery, which runs the risk of jangling or hitting your model in the face, and wearing strong perfume. Also, particularly if you are a smoker (but even if you're not), *always* have mints or gum on you while on a job and wash or sanitise your hands thoroughly before each and every client. You will be entering someone's extremely personal space while you work so you want to be as professional, hygienic, and inoffensive as possible. It's like Maya Angelou said, "I've learned that people will forget what you said, people will forget what you did, but people will never forget how you made them feel."

Finally, what makeup you wear is entirely of your choosing – some artists wear none, while others simply cannot be seen without a full face and a smoky eye! Feel free to show off your personal style in this regard anyway you like but don't feel that just because you're a makeup artist you need to have a perfect full face at all times.

CHAPTER TWO - GAINING EXPERIENCE

Here's where the list of endless possibilities really start to open up before you. I'd say the top three ways to initially build experience as a makeup artist are:

1. Study a makeup course
2. Work on a beauty counter
3. Assist an already established artist

Study

You do not need to have a qualification to work as a makeup artist in the UK and completing a course will certainly not give you the guarantee of a job at the end. In the US, makeup artists need a license to legally be able to work, whereas in the UK, you don't. So obtaining a degree is not mandatory by law, but it is a good option if you'd like to build confidence or simply take some time to learn your craft.

Studying is a tricky one for me to advise on because (particularly in London) there are so many dodgy "schools" offering sub-par makeup courses that'll drain your savings and give you absolutely no value in return. They'll have teachers who don't actually work as makeup artists, issue unrecognised qualifications or no one will have heard of the school so your certificate will be essentially useless out in the real world.

Courses can also be prohibitively expensive - up to tens of thousands of pounds - and offer no true guarantee of employment afterwards. I know of so many artists who committed to (and shelled out for) full three year undergraduate degrees in makeup and tell me they regret going into debt over it, "wasting" so much time in a classroom rather than just going out and starting to build their career, and not being given the aftercare or important industry contacts their schools so confidently promised upon enrolment.

But on the other hand, if you find a **good** course,

it can give you fantastic knowledge of how to work with clients, scientific stuff like skin anatomy, working in a salon/on a counter, selling products, and of course practising makeup in a supportive, controlled environment. Plus, if you ever wanted to become a teacher, you have that piece of paper as proof of your qualifications to take that next step.

I think the key with studying makeup is doing a *ton* of research into every single school offering courses you're interested in and making sure that you are wisely investing your time and money. Be sceptical and don't make any rash decisions. Speak to former students about their experiences. Think about what you want to achieve from the course, what you will get for your money, and what it will offer you in the long run. Also, in the bigger picture, how does it help you achieve what you outlined in your business plan?

My point is, don't feel you *have* to do a super long course to "make it" (despite what these schools will tell you) - after all, Pat McGrath is arguably one of the world's most talented, successful makeup artists and she's completely self-taught, and she isn't alone. Again, there are a million ways to break into this kind of work and it's just all about finding what's right for *you*.

A final word on this topic: I'd hope this would be obvious but do avoid Groupon "makeup course" deals like the plague. I've never seen a reputable school advertise on there. Would you want a makeup artist working on your skin to just have some cheap Groupon qualification…? Didn't think so.

Different Types of Courses

Master Classes/Workshops
Both MAC and Illamasqua offer bite-sized courses in specialised areas, e.g. example how to do drag makeup or Asian bridal looks. MAC requires you to be a member of their pro membership programme to attend (see "Chapter Eight – Pro Discounts" for information on how to

apply) plus you typically pay a small fee on top of this. Illamasqua's classes are available to all but they also charge a small fee.

Find Out More: Illamasqua (*www.illamasqua.com/school-of-makeup-art.list*); MAC master classes are invite only.

Short Course
LCF (London College of Fashion) and AOFM both do reputable, well-reviewed courses in makeup artistry across a range of specific topics. They both are renowned for having excellent teachers who actually consistently work in their industries, and can be a good jumping off point if you're just looking for a short-term course to get you started.

Find Out More: London College of Fashion (*www.arts.ac.uk/fashion*); AOFM (*www.aofmakeup.com*).

Medium Course

More traditionally thought of more for beauty therapists and hairdressers, NVQs are also slightly lengthier courses in makeup artistry where you spend a little longer studying (typically around one full school year) to obtain a National Vocational Qualification. These are especially handy to have completed if you're looking to some day work in a salon or teach makeup.

Find Out More: Google "NVQ makeup artist course (city/town name)" to discover which colleges nearest you offer a suitable programme.

Long Course
Bachelor (BA) degrees are available nowadays in makeup artistry, too. LCF, among other top universities across many UK cities, offer the more intensive, lengthy courses if you'd prefer to invest more time studying. There are many different courses focusing on several industries, i.e. film or fashion.

Find Out More: Google "makeup artist BA degree (city/town name)" to discover which universities nearest you offer a suitable programme.

Work

Another way of gaining experience is to find a beauty counter to work for. This will give you a fantastic opportunity to practice on all different skin types/tones, improve your technical skills, make some contacts and friends in the industry, build up your kit with quality products (hello staff discount!), and earn some money at the same time.

Find a company you love or who most closely aligns with your personality and/or style of artistry. For example, companies like MAC and Illamasqua are ideal for those who love colourful, editorial style makeup, whereas somewhere like Clarins or Chanel would perhaps suit someone **with a more classic, sleek style.**

Keep in mind however that these jobs are 95% about sales. Yes, you are around makeup all day but you will have strict sales targets you'll need to achieve just like anywhere else. If you under perform, you may be asked to leave. It can be an extremely cutthroat world and certainly isn't for everyone. Just remember when embarking on this path that at the end of the day, it is still a retail job and align your expectations accordingly.

How to Get a Job at MAC

As a former MAC employee (many moons ago), one of the most common questions I get asked from young girls wanting to enter the industry is, "how do I get a job at MAC?" So I thought it might help those interested to hear exactly what goes on during the interview process, with some little tips and tricks to help you get your foot in the door!

This is specifically related to how MAC hires their staff; it will not necessarily apply for other companies, as everyone has their own recruitment process. Also, keep in mind that it can take a long time to get a job at MAC and you'll need to put some legwork in, but the good news is that there are almost always vacancies available somewhere.

So let's break down each stage of the interview process for you now.

Step One: Apply Online
Check the MAC careers page and fill out an online application. It's a multiple page web form that will ask you for your contact details, employment history, education history, rough knowledge of the brand, personal favourite MAC products, and so on. It should take you around 45 minutes to complete.

Step Two: Telephone Interview
If you are successful, you will receive an automatically generated email within a day or two (during busy times, it may take longer) inviting you for a telephone interview. The email

will be sent from an Estee Lauder address, as they own MAC, so don't get confused over this. The email will provide a telephone number for you to call whenever you are ready; there's not a specified time slot or deadline for you to call but obviously the sooner you call, the better.

Once you are ready to call the number, you'll be connected to a friendly member of the Estee Lauder recruitment team who will first outline the phone interview process for you. As they will ask you further questions about the brand and your knowledge of it in the interview, they offer you the opportunity to hang up and take 15 minutes to study up a bit before continuing. Obviously just decline this option, as it looks better if you are ready to go ASAP! I can't say whether they would mark points *against* you if you took the offer of extra study time but it looks more like you already know tons about the brand if you're ready and raring to go right away. Plus, now that you are aware they'll ask this of you, try to get any research you need done before you call so you are 100% prepared.

Some topics you might want to research are:

- The history of the brand
- MAC's charitable involvements
- Best-selling products
- New releases (including the actual collection names)
- Some Senior MAC Artists whom you admire
- Recent fashion shows MAC sponsored

So once the telephone interview begins, it's really just in the same style as a standard face-to-face interview in that they'll ask questions like, "Why do you want to work for MAC?"; "What do you know about the brand?"; "Have you studied makeup?"; " What can you tell me about the charities MAC is involved with?"; and so on.

They'll also ask you about your personal makeup style, retail-related questions such as how you'd approach a issue with an unhappy customer or working in a team to achieve goals, how you would link sell or assure you meet sales targets given by your manager. They will ask for concrete examples, so don't give vague answers like, "I'm a team player who likes to work in a shop". HOW are you a team player? Do you have an example of how you displayed this in a previous job? Tell them!

The phone interview only takes around 10-15 minutes on average (depending on how long your answers are). Once the agent is done with the questions, they will put you on hold for a short time and then come back to you to let you know if you passed or failed. If you passed, they will send your details to the relevant Area Manager to get in touch with you directly and they'll also go through what the next steps will be so you know what to expect in the next stage of the interview process.

Step Three: Face to Face Interview
The amount of time you wait for your in-person interview to be scheduled can vary drastically. Some people are contacted by a manager after

just a couple of days; for others it takes months. I once even heard of it taking half a year for a friend of mine! Also, you may not be contacted from a manager from the actual store you will be working in; it could be an area manager who travels between stores or a manager from a completely different store to the one you applied for. Don't panic; it's more just a matter of who they have available at the time to conduct interviews.

Now, once you get a date for your face-to-face interview booked in, show up like you already work at MAC. By that I mean wear all black (yes, even your shoes, I got picked at for that in my interview) and have your makeup done like you would if you were there for a real day of work. Don't be afraid to show off your personal style - MAC loves that kind of stuff. If you have blue hair, cool! Piercings? No problem. That's one of the great things about their company.

Bring along a portfolio or some examples of your work if you have them, an extra copy of your CV just in case, and anything else you've been specifically asked to bring along. You won't need makeup or brushes or anything.

This interview stage is pretty much identical to the phone interview in terms of the types of questions they ask you. However you'll get the chance to show off your makeup work if you have any examples. Even if it's just examples of different makeup styles you've done on your own face or work you've assisted on, bring it along and talk them through each look to show your relevant experience (but in the case of assisting work, be *very* clear that it is not your own work - do not lie and claim it as your own because you *will* be found out).

Other than that, this stage is pretty straightforward and will only take around 30-45 minutes total for them to meet with you and conduct the full interview. It can be a little annoying repeating all the information you've already given twice before (first online then over the phone), but understand that your details have to pass through so many people's hands and it's just part of their process. Plus, you'll be a pro at answering the questions by now!

Step Four: Makeup Test
If you've been successful, you will be called in for the final stage of your interview process, which will be a test of your makeup skills. Like in step three, you may be called by any random manager or do your test in a store that may not necessarily end up being your own if you do start working for them. Again, don't worry about this. It's just how they do things sometimes.

An important point about this stage is that you will need to bring your own model - MAC cannot and will not provide this for you. It can be a bit annoying because the interviews always seem to take place mid-week and of course it can be hard to find someone available to accompany you (who also has nice skin and Kate Moss-esque looks which, let's face it, totally makes your work look more awesome!)

Once again, show up dressed as if you already work there (this is of extra importance this time, as you will be on the shop floor and in front of customers). You don't need to bring your portfolio this time, however you will need to bring your brushes. Upon arrival, go up to the counter and let them know you're there for a makeup test and they will fetch the manager out to meet you right on the shop floor where you will conduct this final stage of the interview process.

So when I did the interview years ago, there were two parts to the test:

1. Fulfil a customer's needs by completing a full face makeup look
2. Execute two different makeup styles of your own choosing, focusing on just two small areas (i.e. eyes and lips, or whatever you choose)

For the first one, the manager will ask you to go away and browse around the store while they brief your model on what to do. Your model will be shown a few MAC face charts of standard makeup looks like smoky eyes, retro red lips, etc, and will be asked to choose one for themselves. Once they've chosen, you'll be called back and you basically enter into a role-play with the model as your pretend customer. Forget you know this person and treat them as you would a customer – it doesn't have to be super formal but do take it seriously.

The idea of this task is to ask them probing questions about what they're looking for and consulting with them so you get a clear idea of the look they have chosen from the face charts; you have to extract little hints from them about what look they want. The aim is not really to test you how close you can get the makeup to the chart, more about how you interact with the customer, investigate their needs, and problem solve. So be sure to make a point of asking the standard questions like, "describe your skin type for me" and "what coverage level of foundation do you like: sheer, medium or full?", as well as talking through what each product will do for them as you go.

After the consultation with your model, you'll go around the store and pick as many testers as you need off the shop floor to achieve their desired look. Important note: BE HYGIENIC! Undoubtedly the manager will remind you of this before you set out to gather testers, but remember to sanitise products and use spatulas to decant products where appropriate. You will be watched very closely on this.

Once you go back to your model/customer, get started right away because you're on a time limit (approximately 30 minutes to make up the full face). Upon completion, the manager will take some notes on your work and then you're on to the next part of the test.

This is where you have free reign to do what you like so try to think of some ideas before you get to your test (and practice on your model if possible to help you speed up on the day). You'll be asked to pick two areas to show off some kind of skill; for example, at the time I did my test, graphic liners were all over the runways so I decided to do that on my model, as it showed off both my technical skill and knowledge of current fashion trends. You will be given a two-product limit per look so keep this in mind when thinking of inspiration (all I used for my graphic liner was "Blacktrack" gel liner so don't feel pressured to use two if you don't need to). The two mini looks you choose are entirely up to your creative direction, your model has no say on this part.

You get around 10 minutes per mini look and once you're done you need to explain a little about what you've done and why you chose to do it. This is a good chance to throw in references to other makeup artists, trends (particularly MAC-related ones), fashion designers, and so on.

After that, your makeup test is done! However you aren't finished just yet; you need to do yet another sit-down interview with this manager first. Your model goes away at this point, they are no longer needed. It's basically the same questions as your phone and face-to-face interview - why do you want to work here, what experience do you have, how will you benefit the team, etc.

And then once you've answered all their questions, you have finally officially completed the entire MAC interview process! Now it's simply a waiting game to hear if they want to hire you. You won't be told at this final stage if you passed or failed; you'll need to wait to be contacted by a manager at the store you'll be working at if successful.

This is the standard, formal way of applying; however if you have a friend already working on the counter and you know of a vacancy at their store, it's also possible to skip the first two interview stages and just go right to interviewing with their manager and doing a makeup test with them. I also knew of some people who just walked into a store they liked, asked about vacancies even without having contacts within the staff, and getting a job just by being in the right place at the right time (and being qualified, of course). So it really is a case of YMMV (Your Mileage May Vary).

Even if the above step-by-step guide isn't every single person's experience when applying for MAC, the overall gist and questions will be the same so just do your research on the brand and practice your makeup skills and you'll do fine.

--

Another option for work is to find a salon that offers makeup services to clients in addition to their other treatments. Like at MAC, you won't technically be a freelance artist so you won't need to worry about things like insurance or registering as self-employed just yet (unless you are working on private clients on the side as well). Instead, you will be employed directly by the salon and they take care of payroll as in other, more traditional jobs.

Usually, however, you'll need to be able to offer the salon other skills than just being able to apply makeup. If you're getting into makeup artistry from a beauty therapy background, this can be an extremely helpful advantage. If you are certified in things like waxing, massages, or even hairdressing, you'll be a more well-rounded, bankable candidate for the salon to employ. It might be worth researching the salons in your local area to see what they have to offer; even if they don't offer makeup services per se, it can be a great education in working with clients in a beauty-related industry.

Assist

This one can be a little tricky if you don't have any prior experience or photos of your work. However don't be put off if you fall into this category because I know of many artists who took on their long-time assistants with absolutely zero experience under their belt and trained them from the ground up.

Assisting, for those who don't know, is where you accompany an already established artist on one of their jobs and help them out; it's essentially like an apprenticeship, though not as defined or accredited. Assisting could be anything from simply just carrying the senior artist's kit, fetching coffee and cleaning brushes or getting stuck in and actually applying makeup on models yourself.

The advantages of assisting are unparalleled - if you become one of the artist's regular assistants, it could eventually lead to them passing on amazing jobs to you (once they've trained you up to a level they're satisfied with) or them hiring you as their First Assistant and paying you a monthly retainer fee to be on call for them at all times. Not just that, you have the potential to make some great industry contacts and learn what set life and etiquette is like on high-end jobs that you otherwise would have no access to. And best of all, you get a front row seat learning techniques and product recommendations from an experienced, highly skilled artist.

It can be exhaustingly hard work, however. Long hours and low pay are prevalent. Assistants should *always* be paid (and never, ever pay someone to assist them on their job; if they are asking money from you - run) but unfortunately not every single job is going to pay the big bucks. Sometimes an assisting job might just be "expenses only", which will cover your travel and lunch expenses. This is particularly true when you are initially building that relationship with the artist. In these situations of low remuneration, it's important to ask yourself what you would gain from assisting on the job: is the artist so skilled/famous that you'll learn a lot from them and potentially boost your career in the long run? Do you admire their work? Or are they an unknown, unsigned artist with a questionable portfolio and seemingly no recognisable relationships within the industry? You be the judge.

To get an assisting gig may take some time and certainly will take a *lot* of emailing and reaching out to people. Research what artist agencies are in your area and contact them to let them know you are available for assisting work, or contact the artists you admire directly (no, not in an Instagram or Facebook comment; compose an actual professional email to send them and ensure you double check your spelling before sending). With each and every email or call, personalise it for whom you are speaking to. If talking with an agency, know which artists they have on their books and what specific work they've done (but of course be open to assisting anyone, if given the chance). And when contacting an artist, make personalised references to their work and explain why you'd be a great assistant.

Example Email

"Hi (AGENT NAME),

I'm a makeup artist who's looking to gain experience assisting, and I wanted to enquire as to whether your books were open for any new assistants?

I recently assisted [ARTIST] on set for an upcoming BBC period drama entitled, "War Sisters". I helped on crowd scenes and SFX for the key talent. I'm a hands-on assistant, not afraid of long hours on set, and I make a fantastic cup of tea!

As a long time follower of [AGENCY ARTIST]'s work, I strive to work in the same TV drama field as he/she does, so would welcome to opportunity to assist them but I'm happy to assist wherever I might be needed for any of your signed talent.

Please find attached a few examples of relevant work of mine, and let me know if you have any questions.

Thank you for your time and I hope to hear from you soon.

*Best wishes,
(YOU)"*

The key with assisting is being flexible. The more flexible you are, the more last minute jobs might come your way, your reputation as an assistant will grow, and you'll get more and more assisting work. You might even end up getting selected to be an artist's First Assistant who gets to travel with them internationally and support them with their big jobs or shows.

When emailing agencies, understand that nine times out of ten you will not receive a reply. It doesn't necessarily mean they don't like you – it could simply mean they're experiencing a busy time at their office, or they don't have any jobs for you, or a plethora of other reasons. I once got contacted out of the blue from an agency I'd emailed almost *two years* prior; they'd saved my details, even though I never heard a peep from them at the time, and contacted me when they finally had something suitable for me come up.

So like everything in this line of work, it's all about patience and persistence!

Tips on Being a Good Assistant

Each artist will be completely different and have their own unique working style. Before you go on your first assisting job with a new artist, be sure to ask them/their agency what they'd like you to bring on the day – often you won't be required to bring anything but they might like you to bring your brushes or a small kit. Be sure to bring your own lunch and bottle of water, as this might not always be provided for you (and it'll seriously suck being stuck in a studio all day in some business park in the middle of nowhere with no access to food, trust me).

Here are some good general rules to get you started:

- Remember that you are there for your senior artist, nobody else; stay near them and be ready for action at all times
- Don't assume anything, i.e. don't just pick up brushes and start cleaning them – the artist might not have been done with them and you've just washed away the colours they were using! If in doubt, ask what they'd like you to do (preferably at the beginning of the job)
- If you haven't been given any direct orders, just observe the work they are doing (in case you need to replicate the same makeup on another model or touch up the work on set later)
- Ensure their work station is kept clean and tidy, but don't hover or get in the way of them working
- Make sure your senior artist is well hydrated throughout the day; offer to get drinks or bring food (especially if they don't have time to eat, which is very often the case)

- Don't hand out your own personal business cards to *anyone* on set; if someone wants to contact you, tell them they can get your details through your senior artist
- Don't ever claim the work you've assisted on is your own; be up front that you were assisting such-and-such artist if you make reference to the job anywhere
- Once you get to know the artist's working style, try to pre-emptively prepare products you know they'll need next

Always try to communicate with the artist to find out what they expect of you and remember that it is not your job or client - you are there only to make your senior artist's job run smoother, nothing else.

In summary, when building experience, I think the best thing to do is some kind of combination of all three: study, work and assist. You don't have to do them all at once but if you chip away at each area, you will undoubtedly begin to notice a solid foundation being laid for a successful career in makeup pretty quickly and finding which areas you're naturally drawn to.

CHAPTER THREE - STARTING YOUR KIT

We all would love to start out with a fully stocked kit with Chanel, Bobbi Brown and Armani but the stark reality of being a poor, start-up freelance artist is that you have to work with what you can afford in the beginning (besides, as a newbie you very often won't know how to use super high end products to achieve the best results yet anyway so it'd be a waste of money and product).

If you do a makeup course, very often a starter kit and brush set will be provided for you at the start – these are fine for now and you can just build from there. If you're starting from scratch, however, below are a few brands with lower price points that can get your kit started. See also "Chapter Eight – Pro Discounts" for how you can obtain industry discounts from participating brands.

Discount Brands

Makeup
- MEMI Makeup (*www.memimakeup.com*)
- MUA (*www.muastore.co.uk*)
- Sleek (available in Superdrug)
- Collection 2000 (available in Superdrug),
- Saturated Colour (*www.saturatedcolor.com*)
- Rimmel London (available in Boots & Superdrug)
- Maybelline (available in Boots & Superdrug)
- Inglot (*www.inglotuk.com*)
- e.l.f. (*www.eyeslipsface.co.uk*)
- W7 Cosmetics (available in Asda)

Brushes
- Real Techniques (available in Boots & Superdrug)
- Zoeva (*www.love-makeup.co.uk*)
- Crown Brush (*www.crownbrush.co.uk*)
- Sigma (*www.sigmabeauty.com*)
- MUA

- Sleek
- e.l.f.
- Eco Tools (available in Boots & Superdrug)
- Bdellium (*www.love-makeup.co.uk*)
- Cozzette (*www.gurumakeupemporium.com*)
- Royal & Langnickel (*www.beautyuk.royalbrush.com*)

Lashes
- Ardell (available in Boots, Superdrug and on Amazon.co.uk)
- Eldora (*www.eldorashop.co.uk*)
- Eyelashes Direct (*www.eyelashesdirect.co.uk*)
- Eylure (available in Boots & Superdrug)

Avoid buying makeup or false eyelashes from eBay or Amazon that is unbranded, as often vendors buy cheap products from China (who don't have the same safety regulation standards as we do in the UK). The products are usually useless and potentially unsafe to use on the skin, so only go with reputable brands from recognised retailers, even if it costs a little more. You know that unbranded eye shadow palette with, like, hundreds of bright colours you've had your eye on from eBay or Amazon because it only costs a fiver? The colour payoff is basically like using children's pavement chalk on someone's skin, i.e. non-existent, and you'll be wasting your money. Spend that little bit extra for a reputable brand, trust me.

The trick with a start-up kit is to get a little bit of everything that enables you to work on any skin tone for any brief from any client. The essentials you'll need are:

- Skincare products (cleanser, toner and moisturiser – for a variety of skin types; if in doubt or on a budget, buy a range that's for sensitive skin)
- Brushes
- Disposables (mascara wands, cotton pads, cotton buds, baby wipes and tissues)
- Foundations (all skin tones)

- Eye shadow palettes (natural shades as well as colourful shades; avoid any with extreme shimmer/frost)
- Liners and mascaras (black, brown, plus waterproof options)
- Lip shades (neutrals, reds, pinks, and coral)
- Lip liners (corresponding to lip colours above)
- Blushes and bronzers (again, avoid shimmery or sparkly pigments)
- Brush cleaner

There's obviously a lot more that goes into a fully stocked pro kit, but this should be enough of a bare minimum to get you started. Later as you progress, you can add secondary items like primers, lashes, and improve the quality of brands you stock.

If you are able to save up around £300, I *highly*, highly recommend buying the Bobbi Brown BBU Foundation and Lip palettes. The foundation palette has every skin tone foundation you'll need to start out, plus concealers and correctors, and the lip palette has 54 different shades, which works out to be around £3.50 per colour – a full priced lip stick costs £24 alone! It's well worth the investment, plus Bobbi Brown almost always has a pop up on their website that gives a 15% discount for first time buyers, so it takes a huge chunk of the cost off for you, too. Just think about buying all those individual foundation shades at Boots if you're shy about the upfront cost… you'd very quickly hit the £220 mark (which is the price of the BBU foundation palette) but will have much less to show for it. Plus you'll have something for every client. Consider it!

If you want a bit more professional guidance on what to put in your starter kit, many brands do "student makeup kits" that have pre-selected products in a big bundle to get you started. MAC Pro offers students this option and Camera Ready Cosmetics have a fantastic one that doesn't require pro registration, as the MAC option does.

And of course you'll need something to store them all in – a kit bag! Some makeup artists use regular old suitcases, which are fine, but there are other specialised kit bags available, too. Brands like Zuca and Stilazzi offer popular options. I personally am a die-hard Zuca fan; they're compact, allow me to separate the weight load across the trolley and the backpack (I use both) to avoid back strain, you can use the frame as a seat, the wheels are specialised rubber like rollerblade wheels that make pulling any weight a breeze, and mine has lasted me years and years without fail. But of course, what works for me, might not suit your needs and it is worth shopping around to see what's out there.

The ultimate key to a good makeup kit bag is sturdy, durable wheels, a good supportive frame that can withstand being bashed around from job to job, and a strong telescopic handle. The size or style is doesn't really matter but it should look professional and be well built. Skateboarding brands, like Burton, also do great options.

I always warn people against boxy designs like those "train cases" or the ones that fold out into several layers/compartments. These are a pain to carry around (I speak from very early, misguided personal experience), look unprofessional and simply don't hold a lot. To start with, a cheap black, lightweight suitcase from Primark should suit you fine until your kit starts expanding more and they also have tons of fantastic clear PVC bags to store your makeup in too.

Finding Inspiration

As you build a better kit over time, it can be a good idea to get some tips and ideas from The Greats – see what the top tier makeup artists have in their own pro kits. There are tons of YouTube interviews that give you a sneak peak inside for some inspiration on your own kit, although sometimes you'll need to go hunting for it. To get you started, here are a couple in a series done by UK artist Sali Hughes focusing on top fashion makeup artists:

- Val Garland's Pro Kit (*youtu.be/brGmh-jCnZg*)
- Mary Greenwell's Pro Kit (*youtu.be/n5Q3XWao4fc*)

Fair warning: this will give you *major* kit envy and if you're a shopaholic, the temptation to buy everything they've got may be too overwhelming! Don't get suckered in to buying something you see online just because someone else raves about it; if you can, go to a store and try it out yourself first. I've had so many disappointing products I've spent a lot of money on that I end up never using just because I believed someone else's hype.

Kit Tips & Hacks

Packing and travelling with thousands of products of varying shapes, sizes and consistencies is unfortunately bound to go wrong at some point. But help avoid some common mishaps with the tips and tricks below:

- Double baggy glitter and pigments in small, sealable Ziploc plastic bags; otherwise prepare for a glitter/pigment explosion that you'll never fully be able to clean from your kit
- Buy a plastic bead box from Amazon, eBay, or a hobby store to contain your disposables like cotton pads, cotton buds, mascara wands, and so on
- Mascara wands can be purchased cheaply in bulk from eBay
- False eyelashes can also be bought in bulk online; make sure they are from a reputable brand though
- Tape down any liquid bottles (i.e. Bioderma) you need to travel with to avoid the cap opening mid-transit
- Always keep your business cards in a clean side pocket of your kit somewhere
- Pack straws somewhere where they won't get bent; this is for models to be able to drink without ruining the lipstick you spent ages perfecting

- Decant your foundations from their heavy glass containers into plastic travel bottles from Muji; you'll instantly lighten the load of your kit (or get a well rounded palette)
- Either crush or melt your lipsticks into a compartmentalised Muji pill box or MAC empty palette to save space carrying all those lipstick tubes
- Store all your brushes while travelling in a brush belt, brush roll or a brush tube – any will do, and is simply down to preference
- Put together a small "first aid kit" to bring with you on jobs with things like plasters, Lemsip, tampons, headache tablets, and anti-histamines (for allergic reactions or swelling of any kind from your model) in case you or the talent have any mini-emergencies on set – I go through mine like crazy!
- Always carry a roll of masking tape on you; it's perfect for getting glitter off of skin
- For a cheap moisturiser, hack buy a bottle of glycerin (can be found online or in pharmacies for super cheap) and find a

travel atomiser bottle; mix roughly half water and half glycerin and shake thoroughly. When rubbed into skin, this gives a beautiful, natural glow – and if sprayed directly without being rubbed in, can also be used as a sweat effect!

How to Travel With Your Kit

Regular wear and tear should be expected when transporting your kit around in between clients - particularly if you live in a big city and have a million flights of stairs to navigate through public transport on a daily basis! But what can you do to protect your kit when you need to travel internationally for work?

The very first step is going to your travel carrier's website and finding out exactly what their passenger baggage restrictions are. Say if you're flying with EasyJet – they will have their rules about weight restrictions and the like clearly listed so you'll know how much you can bring. It varies wildly from company to company and tends to change often, so this is extremely important information to find out; don't just assume anything. Secondly, find the official rules for travelling with liquids (I'd list them here but they seem to change frequently also so it's best to refer to the official .Gov website at *www.gov.uk/hand-luggage-restrictions/overview*).

You'll have two bags to plan for: your checked suitcase and your cabin hand baggage. In your carry-on bag, pack as many expensive, non-liquid items as you can. These will be things like eye shadow palettes, blush or bronzer palettes, pencils, *all* your brushes, and so on. In your checked suitcase you'll put all your liquids and items that otherwise can't fit in your handbag. Try not to put anything super expensive that you couldn't live without (or not be able to do your job without upon arrival), but obviously there's always a certain amount of risk that you just have to take when flying with your kit. If you're insured, as we outlined in Chapter One, you will be fine but obviously you want to minimise the risk of losing or damaging items as much as possible.

When it comes time to pack for your big trip, go down to Poundland or your local Post Office shop and buy some rolls of bubble wrap. The more the merrier! Wrap up every single product in bubble wrap, and then package them in between your clothes in the suitcase as an extra barrier. I also bubble wrap the more delicate hand baggage items, just to protect against bumps and knocks during travelling. I secure all bubble wrap with tape just to ensure they stay wrapped in place protecting my delicate items.

An extra precaution to take is to (if you haven't already) double Ziploc bag products that like to explode such as glitter, pigments, or spray cans. Tape the lids down of any liquids like cleaners or toners so you don't open your suitcase to a soaking wet kit. And if you need to take care of nails for your job, pack a basic nail kit in your suitcase with pre-painted stick on nails and nail stickers (not glue, the cheap stuff you get in nail packs is so bad for nails) in case your model has unsightly natural nails. This also saves you travelling with nail polishes, which seem to love to self-implode in pressurised airplanes.

Finally, all this intensive packaging will take a long time to unpack upon arrival at your destination, to have your kit de-bubble wrapped and ready to go for your client. So ensure you leave yourself enough time to both unpack and then repack when you fly back home. It sounds obvious, but it can take a really long time, so just be prepared.

Bon voyage!

CHAPTER FOUR - BUILDING A PORTFOLIO

Your portfolio will show the world (and most importantly, potential clients) what you can do as a makeup artist. It will be an on-going work in progress and you should constantly be striving to improve the quality of your portfolio; even high-level artists never stop developing their portfolio.

Test Shoots

When first starting out, you'll get pictures for your portfolio through 'testing'. This is where a group of artists get together to collaborate on a photo shoot that isn't necessarily for any specific publication or purpose, but it's a chance for you all to test out some creative ideas and (hopefully) get some quality pictures of your work to put in your portfolio.

For example, a photographer might want to try out a new lighting style he's learned about; a hair stylist might be interested in attempting a crazy runway look; and you might want to trial run some new products or create an experimental makeup look to improve your technique. You can all work together to produce images for everyone's book so that everyone benefits.

There are many, many websites out there where you can create an online profile with images of your work and some information about you. A popular example is a website called Model Mayhem (*www.modelmayhem.com*); there are others out there if you search for them but this seems to be the one with the largest, most active community. It's free to join and you can connect with thousands of other people in your area who are interested in testing.

Another way to find people to work with is to look on Facebook. There are a plethora of groups on there aimed solely at creative talent across a range of industries. Popular ones for London include the "LCF Fashion Network" and the "London Hair and Makeup Artists" groups.

People post there daily with paid jobs, tests, and more. It's a great way to get connected with others in the same industry and get tips from other artists.

Side Note: Staying safe while working as a makeup artist is of huge importance, as you're often working in foreign, private locations with people you don't know. When working with new people, make sure you *always* tell someone where you are going, as well as the contact details of who you've arranged to meet and what time you're expected to be finished. I doubt you'll ever run into any problems, but be smart about keeping yourself safe when arranging jobs and don't be afraid to walk away from a situation if you get a bad gut feeling. No job is worth potentially being harmed over.

If you or your loved ones are really nervous about you meeting a stranger online, Whats App has a great feature where you can share your location live to anyone of your choosing for a set amount of time – anywhere up to 8 hours (and then you can just add more hours, if need be). You don't have to have Whats App constantly open, the GPS data will just automatically be sent from your phone. The iPhone also has the 'Share My Location' option. This way, if you suddenly veer off from your proposed course from a rogue photogapher turned kidnapper, help won't be far behind (extreme example but it has happened!)

Once you've built up some decent portfolio pictures through testing, the next level to get to is model tests. A lot of budding photographers will forge connections with the top London modelling agencies to take photos of their newly signed girls (sometimes referred to as "new faces" or "development") to gain experience and portfolio pictures for their own book. Model test images are usually very simple, natural portraits or commercial-style shots, so while you likely won't be getting to experiment with crazy makeup, it's a great chance to get higher quality photos in your book (because in all honestly sites like Model Mayhem can be very hit-or-miss in terms of quality work). It's a great way to learn how to perfect skin and do natural makeup for the camera.

After you have a good beginner's portfolio in the works with some examples of both natural and creative makeup, you can start to try and get some low level editorials under your belt. An editorial is a magazine spread with some kind of creative narrative and usually you get to do some more advanced, stylised makeup. Perhaps some of the people you've already worked with on test shoots will have some small online magazine connections to get you started, or you can simply start to email photographers who you can see do editorial work and who are roughly on your level. The trick is actually to always aim to work with someone *just* above your level in terms of quality, which will in turn take your work to a higher level.

Then once you have some good test shoots and editorials to display in your portfolio, you should start to be a bit more picky about which collaborations you choose to do and also learning to edit your portfolio – get rid of all those super old photos that brings the quality of your book down. As the saying goes, your book is only as good as your weakest image. This is what I mean by always striving to improve your portfolio; the photos should always be changing for bigger and better things to show off your skill and reflect your progression as an artist.

Building a portfolio isn't going to take just a few weeks; it can take years to build up a book good enough to start working with skilled creative people – and decades to work with the absolute top players in your industry. You just have to be patient and put in the hours; there are no shortcuts in our line of work!

A final word on portfolios – in the old days of being a makeup artist, you had to have a physical, traditional portfolio book to carry around with you. Nowadays, these are much more rare to see, as most portfolios have gone digital. By all means, if you want a physical book with printed, high quality prints of your work - go for it! Just know that it isn't mandatory and putting together a sleek portfolio on your tablet is just as acceptable these days.

Working For Free – When Tests Aren't Tests At All

You'll soon discover, once you build some experience and gain some "street smarts" within the industry, that there are unfortunately a lot of people who will try to get you to work for free by telling you a shoot is a test shoot… when really it isn't.

When I first started out, I was taken advantage of many times by sneaky people who basically wanted a makeup artist but didn't want to pay for one, so they would assure me it was a collaborative shoot, nobody was getting paid, etc. But then you turn up to the shoot, you're given a very concrete brief (with no room for your own creative input; they want you to do the makeup how *they* would like, which is not how a test should be) and then you discover it's actually for someone's "start up clothing line" where they'll be using the images on their website to sell products.

This is appallingly common and only seems to be getting worse these days; even some large high street brands have been caught out asking for unpaid labour from makeup artists in recent years. So it's always important to always be savvy when applying for work.

Your typical "sneaky" job postings always seem to look something like this:

> *"Calling all experienced makeup artists! We are an upcoming British accessory brand whose designs have been seen on Rihanna, Katy Perry and Lady Gaga, and has featured in major editorials for Elle and Harpers Bazaar – to name but a few! We also provided many looks in Beyoncé's latest video! We are shooting a colourful new collection and need the best*

team on board. Do you have what it takes??

This is a fantastic opportunity to get your name out there and get some great exposure in the industry. Unfortunately we cannot pay but we will credit you on social media and it may lead to further work."

So let's break this down. They want an "experienced" makeup artist for a so-called "upcoming" brand… if it's so new and un-established, how has it been so wide spread amongst all these celebrities and publications already? Sounds like they've been around for a good few years at least (either that or they're just outright lying about their credits). Even if they haven't, what they're asking for is professional images shot of their product to help sell it and this should be paid. Always.

It's understandable why artists fall for these jobs, as they do make them sound so exciting and, hey, even if it's not paid you'll definitely get some fantastic commercial shots for your portfolio, right? Plus maybe it'll one day lead to paid work! No. Trust me, you'll only end up being disappointed.

The buzzwords that should make you question things always seem to be the same: great exposure, opportunity, and tons of shameless name-dropping designed to impress you without a lick of evidence to back it up.

The best way to avoid these situations is to ask a lot of questions before the actual shoot date – what is the shoot for? Is it being published anywhere? What is the general direction of the shoot and am I free to take creative control with the makeup? Is everyone on the team collaborating for portfolio pictures? Who is the team? Will the images be used commercially in any capacity?

Anyone with nothing to hide will happily answer these simple questions. If you are getting cagey, evasive responses or outright being ignored, I would think twice about working with them. I've given too many people the benefit of the doubt ("Maybe they're just super busy and don't have time to reply to my email!") but ultimately it's never ended well for me so take this as your word of warning.

In 2015, a Toronto-based ad agency, Zulu Alpha Kilo, actually addressed this issue and created a hilarious short video to demonstrate how absurd it is for clients to ask for freebies. It's aimed at the advertising industry but is just as applicable to our industry, too. AdWeek described the video as, "a guy approaches real men and women (not actors) in other businesses and asks them to provide him with a product or service for free, to see if he likes it before committing to more". You can see the video at:
www.youtu.be/essNmNOrQto.

The scenes are so awkward to watch because it starkly highlights the difference between businesses that traditionally have physical premises of operation of vs. our mobile nature of work. Rarely would anyone have the nerve to walk into a café and literally demand a free coffee, as in the video. Whereas the sneaky clients makeup artists often have to deal have no shame in asking us to work for free from behind the safety of their computer screen, I'm assuming because it has no immediate, face to face repercussions like you see in the video above. The video teaches a great lesson in knowing your worth and standing firm – just because you're not a physical store, doesn't make a client's request for free work any less ridiculous and out of line.

Examples of Jobs That Should Be Paid:

- Actor headshots
- Blogger posts (where the blogger is earning money through advertising)
- Anything for a clothing/product brand or company who will be making money off the images
- Stock images
- Album covers

Examples of Jobs That Are OK To Do For Free:

- Test shots where no one is getting paid and simply doing it for portfolio gain
- Editorials (unfortunately these are very rarely paid these days)
- Occasionally assisting if it's for a huge artist that you feel you'll learn a lot from and will open lots of doors, etc. (but don't feel shy about asking if travel and/or lunch expenses can be covered, as this should be a given for assisting)

Don't just accept a job you *know* should be paid because you want the experience or you're desperate for work due to a slow month; this teaches clients that they don't need to pay makeup artists and in the long run you're only making it harder on yourself when all the properly paid jobs dry up or the fees for hiring a makeup artist are driven way down. This is what has really damaged the industry in recent years

– artists undercutting others or working for free entirely on jobs that should be paid.

Be the change this industry needs and refuse to work for free. Don't put yourself in the situation of being the only one turning up on set who's working for free.

What Should A Portfolio Contain?

Top UK makeup artist, Lee Pycroft, did a small YouTube series of videos with her top tips as a high level artist in putting together a portfolio and the information she shares is invaluable. She's the long-time Head Makeup Artist for "Britain's Next Top Model" and consistently works with super famous celebrities like Liv Tyler, Naomi Campbell, Anne Hathaway, and Kate Moss. I highly recommend you give them a watch at:

- Makeup Artist Lee Pycroft Gives Portfolio Advice (*https://youtu.be/YlYyS-_6gLA*)
- Online Portfolio Tips With Lee & Corinne (*https://youtu.be/BB7TttX8qy0*)

The hard rule to go by is that your first image should always be your best shot and immediately make an impact on whomever you're showing it to. Editing is key and making your portfolio too long or having too many conflicting images is a common rookie mistake. There's no set number of images that is right or wrong, just use your best judgement. Test it out on friends and family for their thoughts, or even better, anyone in the industry who you know can give their honest, educated opinion.

Remember that it's okay to have separate portfolios for the different genres of work you do – if you work in areas like bridal or corporate photography, these areas don't really fit into a fashion editorial book and should therefore go into a portfolio of their own. To just cram all your work, unedited, into one portfolio will make it look sloppy and confusing to clients. You want to tell a cohesive story with a portfolio that communicates to customers what your style is and what you can offer them for the job or opportunity they are offering.

Ways to Support Yourself When Building Your Portfolio

You will not be making much, if any, money when you just start out as a makeup artist, mark my words. In fact, the sad reality is, it can take several months or even years to start earning an actual pay check as a freelance artist.

A good way of supporting yourself while you're building your portfolio (and experience) is going down the aforementioned retail artist route. The downside to this, however, is lack of flexibility. You might get an amazing offer from that photographer you've had your eye on shooting with for ages for the most fantastic editorial… but you can't take it because you're booked in for a shift at work and you need to make your rent payment so can't afford to miss any work.

A workaround for this is signing up with a temping agency; in London, there are several dedicated solely to placing staff on beauty counters around the city (some examples to check out: Beauty Consultants Bureau, Estee Lauder Bureau, and Elite Associates). If you're outside of a major city, there may not be beauty-only temping agencies but perhaps you could look into traditional office temping on the side, as it'll give you a more flexible schedule.

Another idea if you have a knack for writing is to write beauty articles for online blogs and magazines. It likely won't pay very much but it could be a small side hustle to bring in some extra pennies each month and is relatively easy to get started with.

Otherwise, see if you can swing a part-time job, whatever you can find, and doing makeup on the side. It might feel impossible in the beginning but if this is what you really love to do, everything will fall into place if you just keep working hard.

CHAPTER FIVE - NETWORKING

You could be the best, most talented makeup artist in the entire world but if you don't have a circle of well-connected industry contacts through continuous efforts in networking, you're not going to go very far. No one will know who you are or what you can offer.

It's a frustrating truth that it is indeed who you know, not *what* you know, that very often gets you ahead in this line of work. It is understandable, of course, as clients don't want to take the chance on working with an unknown artist lest they provide disastrous, unusable results. You really need to take the time to build up those relationships so people hire you time and time again.

Weekly Checklist
Start thinking about networking as a new integral part of your workweek. Set aside a few hours per week to do things like:

- Reach out to new people you'd like to work with (emails or engaging on social media)
- Find upcoming events in your area where you can mingle with industry people (Facebook and Twitter are fantastic for finding things like magazine launches and new product releases)
- Update your social media pages with industry-relevant hashtags, and up-to-date links for people to get in contact with you
- Organise some test shoots with new people
- Email artist agencies to introduce yourself and let them know you're available for assisting
- Contact beauty PR companies to introduce yourself and enquire about their beauty brands to start becoming a familiar name to them
- Design (or hire someone to) some slick new business cards to start giving out to new connections or to place in local businesses

Do some research online for new ways you can network and drive new business your way. There are tons of free resources online you can utilise in this area. Get creative and brainstorm new ways you can introduce yourself to as many new people as possible.

It might help you to create a weekly checklist of networking tasks you'd like to achieve so if you ever find yourself sitting on the computer with some free time, unsure of what to do, you can refer back to it. It could look something like:

	MON	TUES	WEDS
Email 1 New Photographer		X	
Contact 1 New Agency			X
Email 1 New Production Co.	X		

Set yourself some reasonable goals you'd like to achieve, e.g. contacting 3 new photographers and 1 agency per week. The goal is not to get complacent, even if you feel you have "enough" contacts and are working enough as it is. Those people might drop off the face of the planet tomorrow and you'll be left without your comforting, regular clients. It's a constant hustle!

People As Currency

Perhaps I'm phrasing this in a strange way but I tend to think of my professional contacts as a form of currency. It's simply defining and categorising your connections based on what they can "offer" you. For example, the photographer who is always shooting for top publications (great for building editorial work), or building a solid circle of makeup artist friends who pass jobs amongst each other, or the magazine editor who might help you publish that beauty article you've been wanting to get out there. They might not necessarily be the ones providing the paying gigs but they can be just as important in the long run. It's important to analyse what each new contact can bring to the table for you, just as much as what you can provide them (a great makeup artist).

Finding these valuable contacts is all about quality over quantity – not just spamming anyone you find online with the keyword "fashion" on their website. Think back to your business plan and how this new contact might help you achieve your goals.

But keep in mind: sometimes the best contacts come around when you least expect them! It might not always be the obvious candidate so keep your eyes and mind open, and always be ready to network.

CHAPTER SIX - MARKETING YOURSELF

If you don't get your name out there and showcase what you can offer people, you aren't going to get bookings – simple. There are a number of ways and places you can market yourself, however, and as with many things in freelancer life, there isn't always a right or wrong way of doing things. Often it's a case of trial and error to see what marketing techniques work for you in your market.

Branding
Before you do anything, it's of utmost importance to have a strong, clear brand. This doesn't *just* mean having a nicely designed logo (though that's a start), but it's ensuring you put forth a uniform, recognisable image in every avenue you place your business. Aim to create a brand to suit the type of makeup artist you *want* to be.

If you're unsure what I mean about this, take a look at some of your competitor's websites/online presence and compare how they look to each other. What makes the more impressive website look more impressive than its competitor? It's like the difference between Prada and Primark – which kind of market would you like to target your services to? Your overall image will need to reflect that.

Starting with designing a logo and going from there is a good starting off point in creating your overall brand. If you're confident designing a logo yourself, or have a graphic design friend who could help you out for a discounted fee, great! Otherwise there are a number of services online for all budgets where you can hire someone to make one for you. Both *Fiverr.com* and *UpWork.com* have plenty of creative talent to choose from and are great low cost options to get you started.

Once you have a logo, make sure your website and all related materials (i.e. business cards, social networks, business invoices, e.t.c.) use the exact same logo throughout. Needless to say, it'll just make your business look more professional and put together.

Branding can also extend to the type of content you post online, like on your website or on social media. Your website should clearly showcase your type or work and area of expertise as a freelancer, so visitors know exactly what services you offer. In terms of social media, it's things like ensuring you post quality photos of your work on a fairly frequent basis as opposed to simply spamming your followers with useless, re-posted inspiring quote images that have no relation to your business at all.

The idea is to make sure your overall image, how you portray yourself to the world, is sleek and uniform. If you're all over the place with different logos, styles of photos or non-business related content, it can be very confusing and difficult for high-end clients to take you seriously.

Like with everything else discussed so far, there are plenty of free resources online if you'd like to learn further about professional branding. You don't need to be an expert in it, but it might help you wrap your head around what is good branding vs. bad branding if you really understand what it involves for you personally.

Building A Website

Getting a website for your business can cost a lot of money, like I'm talking tens of thousands of pounds. It's insane – but understandable, as your website is what's going to make you money.

The good news is that there are some free options available for portfolio sites these days that are actually decent. A popular one amongst makeup artists is *Format*; or you can simply search Google for "free online portfolio site" for some alternatives. Although I have my own custom built website for my business now, I used Format in the past when starting out and they offer some really great, easy to customise layouts for portfolio-type work that are just fine for starting out.

Once you're working at a higher level, however, it is worth investing in a customised website, as it looks more professional to have a personalised website that isn't just some template layout you've hastily dragged-and-dropped images into. Also with the free portfolio websites, they'll often have their company watermark in the corner of every page on your website leading back to their website, which kind of gives it away that you're using a freebie site.

Finally, don't just set up a business page on Facebook as your "portfolio" and direct clients to that; it looks super tacky and like you don't get enough business afford a website. By all means, have a Facebook page for your business but use it as a means to connect with your followers instead (see "Social Media" below).

Business Cards

Business cards are a must-have as a makeup artist and you should have some packed away in your kit bag at all times. They should be simple, legible and have your contact details like your full name, profession, website address, email address and phone number. And of course, it should include your logo and have an overall design in the same vein as your logo (i.e. if your logo is black and pink, don't suddenly have a random looking orange and yellow business card that doesn't fit in with any of your other branding).

Some good UK based printing companies are *Moo*, *Vista Print* and *Banana Print*. They each have easy to use websites where you can use their customisable templates to create your own – or simply upload a ready-made design if you want to make one yourself (or have one designed for you).

In my experience, Vista Print is a cheaper option where you get more cards for your money and the quality is perfectly fine. But a noticeably higher quality alternative is Moo, who I always print my cards with. If you'd like to try them, you can use my 10% off discount code ("5tqk7z") when making your first order. Otherwise, feel free to shop around and see what other deals companies can offer you, as they often change.

Social Media

The main social networks you'll want to register accounts for your business on primarily are:

- Facebook (a business page, not an individual account)
- Instagram
- Twitter
- Any other relevant websites that pertains to your industry, e.g. Production Base, if you work in Film and TV, or Hitched if you work in the bridal industry

What you post on your accounts is up to you, as it can be a fantastic way to let your own personality shine through, share behind the scenes photos, and directly speak to followers who are interested in your work. But keep in mind that potential clients will also be looking at your social media pages so keep branding strong and remain professional throughout. Always have your contact information and a link to your website visible on each and every page you create online. You'd be surprised how much work you can find through Twitter or even Instagram!

Utilise Instagram's fabulous business tools; this allows you access to data like how many people have viewed your profile in the last 7 days, if anyone's saved your posts, and how many total people saw every one of your posts – it's invaluable in figuring out what content followers like to see from you best (so you can then post more of that rather than the less well received content). It also allows people to call or email you directly from your profile, without having to go via your website.

Going one step further, I recommend installing a "who's following you" app (there are millions of options out there, for both Android and Apple). It makes me feel a little shady but it's a really good insight to suss out fake followers, i.e. those who follow you out of the blue, hoping you'll be flattered and follow back, but are just looking to boost their own follower count (they'll unfollow you within a day, guaranteed – if they don't personally do it, they're using a follow bot that will). It could also be that contact you meet at work that acts super interested in you in person but later unfollows your profile later that evening (hoping you won't notice yet their follower count will still be +1). All these little tactics are a little silly in the grand scheme of things but it just goes to show, there are a million ways to use social media and an app like this simply gives you more control over how you use it and who you interact with. Decide if this is important to you or not! If you really don't care, I suppose it doesn't matter much either way.

Side Note – I don't recommend you using any of these follow bots yourself or, god forbid, buying any followers. Not only is it painfully obvious when someone does this, it stops you from getting any real insight into who your followers are and what kind of content they like. No one is fooled by the account that has 50,000 followers… but their pictures only ever get 20 likes. Take the time and build your following organically; it'll be so much more worth it and will take you further.

Don't just create your profiles to throw random content on them every now and then – really utilise what social media networks have to offer. It's a great way to set up a network and monitor what's going on in your industry by following influential people or other local talent, finding out about new product releases or interesting articles, browsing through hashtags to find makeup inspiration or tutorials, and making new connections. We live in a time of endless opportunity, thanks to the Internet and specifically social media, so you'd be foolish not to take full advantage of these opportunities to progress your business.

Also, once you have a good amount of followers and posts, you might be able to monetise your social media presence by product sponsorships from beauty companies or PR firms. Read on to Chapter Nine to find out more about how to go about this.

Editorials / Show Reels

Another way to get your name out there is to ensure you do a healthy amount of editorials throughout the year to keep driving traffic to your website. People will be driven to your website through editorial credits on the work that you do (often the smaller, online publications or "zines" will post a direct link to your website, which is a fantastic way to drive new traffic to your site).

If you don't do editorial work, another way could be to edit together a show reel of all the video footage you have of your work and sharing it on websites like YouTube or Vimeo. Always remember to link to your website and include contact details for business enquiries on the actual video and in the description box wherever you upload your show reel, so people can find you and get in touch if they like what they see.

If you're a bridal artist, a fantastic way for brides to find you is to shoot a bridal editorial or feature for a wedding blog based in the UK. I don't even do bridal work myself, but I once had a great shoot featured on one of the UK's top wedding blogs and I was inundated with emails from brides literally within a matter of hours wanting to book me for their wedding!

Finally, be sure to set up Google Analytics to link to your website's traffic; it's *invaluable* to see exactly where people are entering your website from. For example, if you can see you got a ton of traffic coming from that top bridal blog you did an editorial for recently then you'll know that's an effective way of getting people to see your work and potentially hire you. On the other hand, if you spent loads of time putting together a show reel but you're getting no "click-throughs" coming to your site, perhaps you're not utilising this marketing technique correctly or you're simply not hitting the right target audience. Either way, it will allow you to review your methods and adjust.

If you have someone building your website for you, ask them to help you set up Google Analytics with the site. Otherwise, you can read about it at *www.google.co.uk/analytics* (don't worry, it's just a small piece of coding you need to add to your site, it isn't too difficult).

Traditional Marketing

This category includes more "real world" marketing techniques. This could include, but isn't limited to, things like flyers, newspaper advertisements, or setting up a stall at a convention targeted at your industry.

Honestly, my personal experience with this kind of offline advertising hasn't been very successful in my particular field of work (fashion). The reason being is that the majority of networking these days is done online, either through email or even somewhere as informal as Facebook, and offline marketing simply isn't hitting my target audience in the most effective way. The fashion industry is full of young talent, who more likely get their industry news online as opposed to, say, a newspaper.

But I believe success with traditional print advertising will depend heavily on your industry. Bridal artists might have great success placing an ad in a bridal magazine (there are so many to choose from) or printing off some pretty looking flyers to place in a local salon. It's another case of being creative and going through the process of trial-and-error to find what works for your business; just don't feel you have to go out and spend thousands of pounds on some heavy duty marketing campaign, as so much of what we do can be accomplished online nowadays.

MLMs

A MLM (or Multi Level Marketing) company are organisations like Younique, Arbonne or Mary Kay where you join the company as a distributor. You are required to buy a bulk order of stock up front and then sell the products on to customers, in theory to make a profit - but make no mistake, in reality YOU are the real customer to these companies.

I'm going to be very blunt on this subject: please don't waste your time or money on them, even if you're desperate for cash when starting out. You will not make money. "Studies by independent consumer watchdog agencies have shown that between 990 and 999 of every 1000 participants (i.e. between 99.0% and 99.9% of all participants) in MLMs in fact lose money", according to Kathryn A. Jones' "Amway Forever" book on the subject. Aside from that, you will cause irreparable damage to your makeup artistry career, because no one will take you seriously after being affiliated with brands like these.

If you still are on the fence about joining one, I highly recommend sitting down one afternoon with a cup of tea and reading through Elle Beau's personal account of her time Younique at *http://ellebeaublog.com/poonique* (excuse the rude name!) She's a girl from the UK who documented her experience in joining the company, all the characters she meet along the way, and ultimately her decision to leave the company including how much she actually made/lost in the end. It's really funny and well written, like a friend talking to you (but with memes included), and it takes you behind the scenes of the actual process one goes through when signing up to one of these companies.

In short, I recommend avoiding them at all costs; it's a slippery slope to go down.

Setting Your Rates

Your "rate" is the amount of money or fee you receive for working a job. Usually, as a makeup artist, these are calculated as an hourly, half-day and full-day rate. Your rate should reflect your experience, skill level, and market you work in.

Posting what my rates are here would be pointless (I get asked this a lot), as we may not be in the same industry or on the same skill level, so therefore we would not be paid the same. Also, rates can fluctuate often so I'd only be dating this book if I included specific numbers.

How you figure how much to charge is – yep, you guessed it – another research mission (sorry!) Here are some ideas of places you can research to find a rate list that's right for you:

- Visit BECTU's website and search for "rates" to view their current table outlining acceptable industry fees for artists

- Search for other, competing makeup artists in your areas to see if they post a price list (this is more common with bridal artists than other industries, who may not list anything at all)

- You can email other artists in your market and outright ask them! Often, for whatever reason, many will not like to disclose this information with you so you could be a little sly and email them as a potential client enquiring about services and their price list. I don't advise lying to anyone but if you're really hitting a brick wall and honestly can't find any idea of what rates are like in your area, it's a little life hack you can utilise

- Ask around in the Facebook makeup artist groups; you're more likely to have someone guide you in the right direction there as it's more informal and friendly

Once you have an idea of ballpark rates people are charging in your industry, you can start to pin down what is realistic for you to charge. You should be basing your rates off your skill level, experience, and market you work in. Artists working in Leicestershire won't be earning the same level as those working in London, simply because the demand for work is lower and the costs of living aren't as high as in the capital – even if your skill level is exactly the same. Also, perhaps this is obvious to most, but do keep in mind you won't be earning the same amount as someone who is already established in your field right away, especially when still building up experience.

You must also be generally aware of the costs of running a business. For example, you'll need to take into account how much things like travel, kit replenishment, insurance, tax bills, web hosting and the like are going to cost you. To put it simply, if you're only charging £30 to do a call-out makeup job where you go to someone's house to get them ready for a party, well you'll spend maybe £10 on travel, £5 on false eyelashes, at least £5 on products you use up. That leaves you with £10 profit… but then you might have a bill at the end of the month for your web hosting, which works out to be £25 so now you're actually negative £15. You will not be able to earn money as a business if you set your rates too low, and will essentially be paying out of your own pocket to do this kind of work, which makes no sense at all.

Be realistic but fair in the rates you eventually set for yourself. That way you'll feel confident telling potential clients your fees when approached for work; if the client is offering something too low where you will be losing money, then don't be afraid to (politely) say so and stick to your guns. In my experience, it's always the clients with the cheapest budgets who will fight to work you to the bone – and it just isn't worth the hassle.

CHAPTER SEVEN – HOW TO WORK FASHION WEEK

This is a big question I am asked very often: how does one go about working at fashion week as a makeup artist?

The important thing to realise is that "fashion week" is really a catchall term used to describe several shows and presentations that occur every September and February in London. Shows are classified as either "on-schedule" or "off-schedule". On-schedule will be the top shows, like Burberry, Vivienne Westwood, or Mulberry – essentially any huge brand whose show is listed on the official London Fashion Week website (*www.londonfashionweek.co.uk*).

Off-schedule can be anything from the more mid-level shows (such as Fashion Scout or Fashions Finest, although one or two Fashion Scout shows are often on-schedule) to any old small time designer hosting a presentation hoping to capitalise on the flock of industry insiders rushing to the city each season.

Obviously it's more lucrative and prestigious to work the on-schedule shows, as they will be for brands that everyone has heard of and will look better on your CV. But no one can just hop right onto Val Garland's makeup team and work these kinds of gigs; you have to build your way up first and the smaller, lower level shows are a great way to prove yourself and get a taste of the supremely manic backstage area. It's not always how people imagine it's like and it can often be thankless, tiring work with stressed out people screaming at you.

But if you'd still like to get involved, a good way to start is to research exactly which artists headed up the makeup teams for previous, recent shows. Make a list of all the artists you can find as well as their respective agencies. Then, a couple months before show season starts, reach out to all the agencies and put yourself forward to be on teams with some examples of your work and any relevant show experience you have.

You might get lucky this way but honestly agencies do get thousands of people emailing them year round wanting the exact same thing. It's very easy to slip through the cracks, no matter how talented you are. It's worth trying, so at least they do have your details on file, but don't set super high expectations.

The best way to do it is to have an existing relationship with the types of artist who keys shows; this is how it happened for me every single season I've ever worked on fashion week (and I've done both low and high end shows). So it really is worth building relationships through assisting and, even if you haven't assisted them in a while, getting in touch with them before the next season starts up to catch up and see if you can be of help on one of their teams.

Bottom line: it's a bit of luck, a bit of who you know, and a whole lot of emailing and patience. Good luck!

CHAPTER EIGHT - PRO DISCOUNTS

Pro discounts are one of the many delightful benefits of being a professional makeup artist. It's a great way for companies to gain repeat, lifelong customers and increase their chance of having influencers be seen using their products. And it gives you a chance to build your kit at a more affordable price!

Below I have compiled an exhaustive list of all the current pro discount schemes available to UK artists, as well as where and how to apply for them.

A-F

BACKSTAGE BEAUTY
- Discount: Told upon application
- Requirements: Told upon application
- Membership Fee: No

- To Apply: Email *hq@backstagebeauty.co.uk* for application form and requirements

BARE MINERALS
- Discount: 25%
- Requirements: Two pieces of professional I.D. dated within the last year, i.e. business card, makeup certification, letter of contract, etc.
- Membership Fee: No
- To Apply: Email *awillars@bareescentuals.co.uk* for an application and return with the required documents

BASE
- Discount: 20% Pro / 10% Student
- Requirements: Dependant on type of discount you're applying for; see their pro discount page for further details
- Membership Fee: No
- To Apply: Obtain application form from website then email

proteam@baseproartists.com with your application and supporting documents

BEAUTY CHAMBER

- Discount: 20% Pro / 10% Student
- Requirements: Told upon application
- Membership Fee: No
- To Apply: email *sales@beautychamber.co.uk* to request an application and find out further details

BELLA PIERRE

- Discount: 20%
- Requirements: General proof of profession documents; refer to their pro discount page for full details.
- Membership Fee: No
- To Apply: Email *katie@bellapierre.com* with supporting documents

BOBBI BROWN

- Discount: 35% Pro / 20% Student
- Requirements: Photo I.D. (x1) and three pieces of professional evidence e.g.

business card listing name and specific profession; editorial page with name credit; contract on production company letterhead; programme or press material with name credit; union card; professional valid licence; or proof of qualifications
- Membership Fee: £15-25 annually, depending on which type of membership you hold
- To Apply: email *bobbipro@bobbi-brown.co.uk* to request an application form, which will be mailed to you along with the full requirements

CAMERA READY COSMETICS

- Discount: up to 40%
- Requirements: Dependant on your industry/experience; see their pro discount page for full details
- Membership Fee: No
- To Apply: Email the required documents and your details to *service@crcmakeup.com*

CHARLES FOX
- Discount: Told upon application
- Requirements: Told upon application
- Membership Fee: Free for the first year; £25 annually thereafter (unless you spend £1,000 or over your first year)
- To Apply: Create an account at *www.kryolan.com* and fill out their online form. You must then post them your evidentiary documents for review

CHARLOTTE TILBURY
- Discount: 30%
- Requirements: Photo I.D., qualification certificate, plus two pieces of supporting work evidence
- Membership Fee: Free
- To Apply: Email *pro.applications@charlottetilbury.com* with your documentation and details; to see exactly what they require, refer to website.

COCKTAIL COSMETICS
- Discount: 20% Pro / 10% Student (participating brands only)
- Requirements: Photo I.D. plus two forms of professional supporting documentation
- Membership Fee: None
- To Apply: Create an account at *www.cocktailcosmetics.co.uk* and then fill out their online application form.

COCO BEAU
- Discount: 10-20% (depending on experience)
- Requirements: Certificate, business card, and one or more pieces of professional evidence
- Membership Fee: No
- To Apply: Create an account at *www.cocobeau.co.uk*, then follow the steps outlined on their website. You'll need to email *admin@cocobeau.co.uk* an outline of your business along with your supporting documents.

CROWN BRUSH

- Discount: 10% Pro / 20-40% Student
- Requirements: Photo I.D. and two pieces of professional documentation, e.g. website link, tear sheet, certificate, e.t.c
- Membership Fee: No
- To Apply: Fill out their online web form

DANIEL SANDLER

- Discount: 20%
- Requirements: Photo I.D. and two pieces of professional documentation
- Membership Fee: No
- To Apply: Fill out the relevant application form on their website and post it to them with your supporting documents

DERMALOGICA

- Discount: 30%
- Requirements: Two pieces of professional documentation
- Membership Fee: No

- To Apply: Email *insider@dermalogica.co.uk* for application form

DINAIR
- Discount: Up to 35%
- Requirements: Two pieces of professional documentation
- Membership Fee: $35 annually (open internationally)
- Requirements: Photo I.D. and two pieces of professional documentation
- To Apply: Fill out their online form

ELDORA LASHES
- Discount: 25%
- Requirements: Two pieces of professional documentation
- Membership Fee: No
- To Apply: Create an account on *www.eldorashop.co.uk* and refer to the discount guidelines, then email *contact@eldora.co.uk* with your supporting documents

GINVERA

- Discount: 30% (but 50% off your first order only)
- Requirements: Website link or two forms of supporting documents as outlined on their pro discount page
- Membership Fee: No
- To Apply: Email *jan@janiro.co.uk* with the required information from the pro discount page, above

GURU MAKEUP EMPORIUM

- Discount: Told upon application
- Requirements: Min. 3 forms of professional I.D.
- Membership Fee: No
- To Apply:
  Email *shop@gurumakeupemporium.com* to request an application form

ODYLIQUE (FORMERLY ESSENTIAL CARE)
- Discount: Told upon application
- Requirements: Copy of CV with two examples of profession, i.e. business card and website. See their pro discount page for full details.
- Membership Fee: No
- To Apply: Email details to *kirsty@essential-care.co.uk*

ILLAMASQUA
- Discount: 20-40% (depending on profession/experience)
- Requirements: Supporting documents dependant on your specific industry; see their pro discount FAQ page
- Membership Fee: No
- To Apply: Fill out their online form along with your supporting documents

INGLOT
- Discount: 20% Pro / 15% Student

- Requirements: General supporting documents of your profession, e.g. business card, tear sheets, e.t.c.
- Membership Fee: No
- To Apply: Visit a store and apply in person

KEVYN AUCOIN

- Discount: 40%
- Requirements: Photo I.D. plus two forms of professional I.D.
- Membership Fee: No
- To Apply: Create an account on their website and fill out their online form

NOTE: Orders are shipped from the US so postage is extortionate, starting at around £60! Therefore it might work out cheaper to order from LoveMakeup.co.uk who do a 20% Kevyn Aucoin discount

LAURA MERCIER

- Discount: 40%
- Requirements: Any high-level supporting documents you have, e.g. agency representation proof on company

letterhead, agency website, union card, or tear sheets
- Membership Fee: No
- To Apply:
  Email *makeup.artists@lauramercier.com* with as many supporting documents as you can find

LONDON BRUSH COMPANY
- Discount: 30% Pro / 15% Student
- Requirements: Photo I.D. plus one proof of profession. Must have min. 2 years experience if applying for Pro; see full requirement details on their pro discount page
- Membership Fee: No
- To Apply: Create an account at *www.londonbrushcompany.com* then send supporting documents to *pro@londonbrushcompany.com*

LOUISE YOUNG COSMETICS
- Discount: Told upon application

- Requirements: Website link, recent call sheets and/or tear sheets
- Membership Fee: No
- To Apply: Email *info@louiseyoungcosmetics.com* with your proof of profession documentation

LOVE MAKEUP

- Discount: 20% Pro / 10% Student (participating brands only)
- Requirements: Proof of I.D. and two forms of professional criteria
- Membership Fee: No
- To Apply: Create an online account at *www.love-makeup.co.uk* and fill out an online form

MAC

- Discount: 35% Pro / 15% Student
- Requirements: Depends on which discount you are applying for; contact MAC directly for further information
- Membership Fee: £25 annually

- To Apply: Call 0800 054 2676 or email *infomacpro@maccosmetics.co.uk* for more information or to ask for an application form; you can also get an application and a temporary discount card on the day in any MAC Pro store (if you meet the requirements)

MAKEUP ATELIER PARIS
- Discount: 30% Pro / 10% Student
- Requirements: Two supporting documents; see their pro page for full details
- Membership Fee: No
- To Apply: Create an account at *www.makeupatelierparis.co.uk* and then fill out their online form

MAKE UP FOR EVER
- Discount: 35%
- Membership Fee: No
- To Apply: email *enquiries@preciousaboutmakeup.com* for an application form & requirements

N-T

NARS
- Discount: 40%
- Requirements: Tear sheets, film or TV credits, agency representation info, proof of union membership, e.t.c
- Membership Fee: No
- To Apply: Email *artistprogram-uk@narscosmetics.eu for* an application form and full requirement details

OBSESSIVE COMPULSIVE COSMETICS
- Discount: 20%
- Requirements: Website and/or business cards, diploma, tear sheets, e.t.c; full details on their pro discount page
- Membership Fee: No
- To Apply: Email *pro@occmakeup.com* for an application form

PAM

- Discount: MUFE (35%), MUD (30%); Louise Young, Bdellium and Joico (20%); other brand discounts may be available
- Requirements: General proof of profession documents
- Membership Fee: No
- To Apply: Email *enquiries@preciousaboutmakeup.com* for an application form and full requirement details

ROYAL & LANGNICKEL

- Discount: Told upon application
- Requirements: None, you just specify which industry you are in upon applying
- Membership Fee: No
- To Apply: Fill out their online form

SARA HILL

- Discount: 30% Pro / 20% Student
- Requirements: One form of photo I.D. plus two forms of proof of profession as outlined on their website

- Membership Fee: No
- To Apply: Email your supporting documents to *info@sarahill.com*

SATURATED COLOUR (FORMERLY NYX)
- Discount: 15%
- Requirements: Told upon application
- Membership Fee: No
- To Apply: Create an account at *www.saturatedcolour.com* and then find "Apply for Pro" under the "My Account" area. Fill out online application form with required supporting documentation

SCREEN FACE
- Discount: 10%
- Requirements: General proof of profession documents (any)
- Membership Fee: No
- To Apply: Enquire in-store with your documentation

STILA
- Discount: 30%

- **Requirements**: Website link & agency representation
- **Membership Fee**: No
- **To Apply**: Fill out their online form

SUPERCOVER

- **Discount**: 25%
- **Requirements**: Depends on if applying for pro or student discount; refer to their website for full details
- **Membership Fee**: £24 annual fee
- **To Apply**: Email *zaf@supercover.co.uk* with your supporting documents

TILT MAKEUP

- **Discount**: 10%
- **Requirements**: One form of proof of profession as outlined on their pro discount page (link below)
- **Membership Fee**: No
- **To Apply**: Create an account on *www.tiltmakeup.com* and then fill out their online form

TWEEZERMAN
- Discount: Told upon application
- Requirements: Professional portfolio showing 5 tear sheets with name credit and a current professional beauty certification (i.e. NVQ)
- Membership Fee: No
- To Apply: Fill out their online application form

U-Z

URBAN DECAY
- Discount: 35%
- Requirements: General proof of profession documents (any)
- Membership Fee: No
- To Apply: Apply in-store to receive your card same day

VICTORIA LOVES BEAUTY
- Discount: 20% Pro / 15% Student
- Requirements: General proof of profession documentation (any)

- <u>Membership Fee</u>: No
- <u>To Apply</u>: Fill out their short online form with required details

YABY

- <u>Discount</u>: 20%
- <u>Requirements</u>: General proof of profession documents; full details available when you fill out an application form
- <u>Membership Fee</u>: No
- <u>To Apply</u>: Create an account on *www.yabycosmetics.com* and then follow their requirements to fill out their online form

Types of Supporting Documents:

Often the brand websites will outline exactly what types of evidence they require as proof you're a makeup artist but for those who are vague or you don't understand what they're asking for, here are some ideas of what you can gather together to show them and their definitions:

Call Sheet – a document outlining the schedule for a shoot/project you're working on, as well as the team details.

Union Card – you can get this easily by joining BECTU (which will also provide you with insurance and other industry benefits, as outlined in Chapter One). This will be a simple membership card showing you're a paying member of the BECTU union.

Tear Sheet – this is an editorial page that has been 'torn' from a magazine showing your name credited as the makeup artist. Nowadays, many online magazines provide this also but obviously it will be a digital "tear" (not really a tear at all) and should still qualify.

Comp Card – this is more of a US term, although you'll find it sometimes on some UK websites when asking for documentation. It's not a business card but rather a larger format card that highlights examples of your work. They're more often seen in relation to models, so you can try Googling "model comp card" to see an example.

Website/Portfolio – self-explanatory. Many companies will not accept Facebook/social media pages as proof, so make sure you have a professional-looking website showcasing your work before applying for discounts.

CHAPTER NINE – HOW TO GET SENT FREE PRODUCTS

Another perk of the job, for certain artists who do a lot of publicised or high profile work, is PR companies will very often want to send you free products. This is something known as "editorial gratis" or simply product sponsorship and many young artists wonder about how you go about it.

Any artist who does a lot of editorial/published work, red carpet, celebrity and TV work, or even things like beauty writing, will be loved by beauty PR companies so it's worth getting in touch with them and extending an introduction if this is the kind of work you do. This is because when an artist has work published, their details will be on the "credit", which is the list of the team members for that shoot/project. If supported by a PR company, you may often see a makeup artist credited as: "Makeup by Jane Doe using Chanel" or some other cosmetic brand name. This usually means they have pre-arranged with

Chanel's PR to place that credit in the publication in exchange for free products to be sent to them. It's a win-win situation because the brand will get "free" (or at least, dirt cheap) advertising and the artist will get free products for their kit.

Start by researching on Google for keywords like, "Beauty PR London" to have a whole list of potential new contacts laid out before you. Not all companies will represent brands relevant to your work, so it is important to do some research about who represents whom and educating yourself on the different brands you may be a bit more unfamiliar with.

The next step is getting in contact (an email is generally preferred) to say hi and either tell them about an upcoming editorial/publicised job you have that they might be interested for X makeup brand or, if you have no suitable jobs coming up, you could simply enquire about if they have an editorial product sponsorship programme in place for makeup artists. This will forge that first introduction and find out how they work, as each company operates differently. They'll be able to send you all the relevant details, i.e. what publications the brand will accept credits for, and which agent takes care of that brand.

An example email could be:

> *"Hi (Agent Name),*
>
> *I'm a makeup artist who has an upcoming shoot for Vogue UK with photographer Tim Walker. I was wondering if (Brand Name) would be interested in a credit for this? It's a two girl editorial with an 'Alice in Wonderland' theme, featuring designs by McQueen.*
>
> *Let me know your thoughts and if this is something you'd be interested in.*
>
> *Kind regards,*
>
> *(YOU)"*

If your work isn't at a very high level yet, you might not even get a reply but it's worth starting to get your name recognised by the companies as someone who shoots higher profile work (as opposed to more private work, such as bridal). If they don't know you, they might ask for further details or just say "maybe next time". It's simply another case of persevering until you find your way in.

If they do want to give you the credit – great! Each company has a different way of sending products; very rarely will they send them before the event unless it is red carpet or celebrity work (as they'll want to get their products in the hands of the celebrities too who will, best case scenario, post online about the brand to their fans). The PR agent will let you know how many products you're allowed to choose – often simply referred to as a "wish list" - and will send them over once you email them the finished editorial/project for review. It's also good PR etiquette to share on social media when you have been sent products, as it reaches a whole other demographic (your social media followers) who may not have seen the publication and you can let them know a breakdown of which products you used and how.

A good way of getting a bit friendlier with the PR teams is to personally deliver or post any physical copies of work if you live nearby that shows the credit you've arranged with them (even if you sent PDF scans already). As a bare minimum, remember to send a thank you email once you receive the gratis products. Bonus points are things like Christmas cards to their office each year to continue a good relationship – don't go overboard and start kissing butt, sending huge bouquets of flowers or anything (maybe some would love that but at the same time it isn't needed and you don't know whom it might turn off). Remain neutral and professional, but don't let them forget you exist.

Once you build some solid PR relationships, you'll find your need to purchase makeup goes way down, which is fantastic! Often companies may even send you free stuff out of the blue, such as new releases, which also helps keep your kit topped up year-round and keeps you on your toes, trying out new products and brands.

Lastly, don't feel shy about contacting PR companies; it's what they're there for and they need you just as much as you need them!

CHAPTER TEN – MANAGING FINANCES

I will be the first one to tell you that I am not a "Math person". I find the world of accounting incredibly dull (sorry to all the accountants out there!) But keeping track of your finances while operating as a business does not have to be a long, arduous process. In this chapter, I'll include some handy management tips to set up an easy-to-maintain accounting system.

Banking

You will need a bank account once you start earning money as a freelancer as you'll want to keep your personal and professional finances separate for tax filing purposes. It's super easy and straightforward to open up a simple current account with any UK bank and that's all you really need. In fact, many banks let you open a new current account online if you already bank with them, and the new account will simply get added to your existing account overview when you log in to your account online. Easy! You can usually rename the account to something like "Business Account" or "MUA", whatever helps you separate the accounts the easiest.

Make a note of your new account number and sort code somewhere safe but handy, so you're able to quickly send it to clients with your invoices. Be sure to activate a debit card for the account and, if you need one, ask for a paying in book for petty cash deposits.

Bookkeeping

Now, how to track all these incoming and outgoing expenses you're starting to accumulate? One solution that I know many artists use is a simple spreadsheet – either in Microsoft Excel or Google Sheets. I personally hate this method though, as it gets way too cluttered and confusing for my simple brain and I prefer having an all-in-one system that can do extra little things like generate invoices and create client profiles and so on.

For this I use an online service called Quick File (*www.quickfile.co.uk*). They used to be free of charge but as of 2016, they changed to an annual membership fee, which was really annoying when I first learned of it, as I'd been happily using them for years up until that point with no issues. However, after researching around all the available cloud accounting management services, their annual membership fee actually worked out a lot cheaper than any of their other competitors. Quick File did give us existing members a few weeks' warning of the switchover to give you a fair chance to export and save all your stored files if you wanted to, but after shopping around and price matching other similar services, I was happy to just pay the new service fee and continue using them.

Side Note - Like the insurance companies I recommended before, I have no affiliation whatsoever with Quick File other than I have used their service for many years and like their interface and the features they offer. There are certainly many other companies you can look at if you want to go this route when keeping your books on an online cloud storage system, you don't have to use Quick File. To compare what else is out there, try searching for keywords on Google like "online cloud accounting" or "online bookkeeping software".

The reason why I prefer an online bookkeeping management site is it's so easy to use and everything has it's place – Sales, Expenses, Bank Account Info – and the Quick File dashboard in particular gives a great graphic chart overview of your monthly earnings/expenses. QF also notifies you if a customer is late with paying and how much money is owed to you. There's also an option to sync your bank account directly too so when you make a purchase or a sale, it'll automatically update your books for you, which is fantastic.

Furthermore, at least in the service I use, there's the option to scan in and attach all your saved receipts to the corresponding transaction. So you have a digital record as backup, as well as the physical receipt in your tax folder at home. Gives you great peace of mind in case of emergencies!

It also has an invoice generating service, where you can customise them exactly how you want it to look including attaching your own brand logo on there if desired.

For me, a simple spreadsheet doesn't do all I want it to do and as I get too many bookings, it gets too convoluted so I prefer having a full serviced program like this that basically does everything for me. It's completely up to you and what you find easiest to work with, however, when selecting a bookkeeping solution for your company. It just took me many years to realise these kinds of websites were in existence, so I wanted to include a couple options for you in this section so you know what's out there and can determine what suits your own business needs.

Chasing Late Payments

Unfortunately you will, at some point in your career, run into clients who cannot or will not pay you for services you have completed. You've sent your invoice, followed up to request an update on payment, and still… nothing. Don't worry because you do have some options at your disposal to getting your rightfully owed money.

Late Payment Fees
If a client is dragging their feet on paying you for a job, you can threaten them with something called "late commercial payment fees". In the UK you are legally entitled to charge a percentage of the total billable amount for every day the client is late.

The Gov website explains, "the law says the payment is late after 30 days for business transactions after either: the customer gets the invoice or you deliver the goods or provide the service (if this is later)."

The interest you can charge is called "statutory interest", which is 8% plus the Bank of England base rate for business-to-business transactions (as of March 2016, it is 0.5% although keep in mind this percentage may change; check the Bank of England website for up-to-date information).

Example

Let's say a company owes you **£1,000** for a job you completed. The total yearly statutory interest you'd be owed **£85** (because this would be worked out as: 1,000 x 0.085 = £85). Divide the £85 by 365 to get your daily interest, which works out to be **23p** a day (85 / 365 = 0.23). After 60 days of non-payment this would work out to be **£13.80** (60 x 0.23 = 13.80), which could be added to the invoice and re-sent to the client with the new amount.

It's never nice to have to threaten late payment fees (and people generally don't take too kindly to it I find, funnily enough) but you are legally within your right to demand them. At the very least, it might be the kick up the butt the company needs to finally cough up what they owe you.

To find out more information about late payment fees, search for "late payment" on the Gov website to find the relevant web pages.

Small Claims Court

If a client still isn't paying up even after you've tried contacting them, politely reminding them of their late payments and maybe even threatening to charge them late payment fees... well then it might be time to take more drastic action.

Making a court claim against a company or person through the small claims court is a quick, easy process that can be completed online. All you do is visit *www.gov.uk/make-money-claim-online* and login with a Government Gateway I.D. (if you don't have one, you can create one there) and fill out the details they ask of you pertaining to the job you completed and require payment for. This is good for amounts up to £100,000 but against no more than two people or organisations.

Basically what will happen is that the courts will look into your claim and you may have to attend a court hearing if the other person/business denies owing you the money. If they are found to be liable, the court can order them to pay (usually they'll be ordered after admitting they do owe you the money or by not responding to your claim). If they still fail to pay, you can ask the court to take further action in collecting the money, at which point they may involve using bailiffs.

I've had to go through this horrible process only once in my career so far and it's incredibly stressful. Luckily, they make the online process very simple and everything was resolved (and paid for) within a week or two. So if you're truly hitting a brick wall with a company, don't be afraid to use this option to get what you are rightfully owed.

Report to BECTU

In case you missed it in the "Insurance" section in Chapter One, BECTU are a UK-based media/entertainment union for freelancers primarily working in the film, TV and theatre industries (though also supporting other areas and slowly gaining ground in the fashion industry also). If you're having problems with a company not paying you for services or asking you to work for free, even if you're not necessarily a member of the union, BECTU may be able to look into it for you. They can contact the offending company with a warning of the UK laws they are breaking, if they are indeed committing an offense. Being contacted by a trade union might scare the rogue company into compliance, so it's always worth seeing if they can help you out.

To find out more information or join, contact BECTU on *info@bectu.org.uk*.

Budgeting

As a freelancer, some months you'll be raking in tons of money and you'll think, "yes now I've finally made it"… but the next, you'll barely be able to scrape together any paying jobs and you'll start to worry that you'll never work again. It happens to all freelance makeup artists and is something you have to be mindful of.

(Actually, a photographer friend of mine explained it as the "2 weeks on/2 weeks off" theory; this is where it seems like you'll be solidly booked for two weeks straight, busy working every day… and then because you've been busy running around doing these jobs, you haven't been networking and setting up your next upcoming jobs, which leads to two weeks of "downtime" a.k.a. you sitting at home doing admin work, trying to set up some new leads).

Keeping an eye on your budget to help you through slow weeks/months can be a lifesaver. You don't have to write up a long, detailed budget of exactly what you will spend your money on; it's more just being conscious of things like, 'Ok I've spent a lot of money on makeup this month, next month I'll be sure to slow things down and save more'. Business won't always be booming and you need to have a contingency plan for when times are slow so you won't be missing rent payments or eating instant noodles for four weeks straight.

CHAPTER ELEVEN – GETTING AN AGENT

So let's say you've done all of this, you've had a great career building for the last couple of years, you've had some success, and now you feel ready for representation. Agents can elevate you to that upper echelon of clients, whether it be bigger commercial brands or higher end magazines.

To start with, be realistic about what *you* have to offer an agency – not just in terms of quality of work but also what clients you can bring to the agency. They're there to make money at the end of the day and if all you can show in your book is some cute editorials but don't really have a solid client base, you aren't worth a whole lot to them. There are lots of makeup artists out there who can do nice makeup, but one who can bring in more money to the agency will obviously be in higher demand.

It's not even just that, it's who you are as a person, how you work with other people, how active you are on social media, how many followers you have, what kind of "voice" you have in the industry, what your niche is, how you personally gel with the agency itself… there are a million variables that can mean the difference between you signing with an agency or remaining solo.

But don't make the mistake of putting agencies on a pedestal and feeling like getting represented by one is the be all end all – if you're having perfectly good success working on your own, then ask yourself what you really want an agent for. Is it help with invoicing and booking jobs? Help reaching that next level of clients? Or are you doing fine with all of the above, and it's purely a status symbol you're after? If it's the latter, just remember that grass isn't always greener on the other side. And if you're doing fine on your own, why give away 20% of your earnings to someone else?

Some anecdotal evidence for you - I have a friend who joined a small, boutique London agency; she was thrilled because she had been desperate to gain representation for the longest time and finally felt that she'd "made it". In the first year of being on their books, guess how many jobs she got through them? One. Turns out, the agency just didn't have the industry contacts they promised and couldn't find their artists work (it wasn't just her). She was just so desperate for an agent that she didn't examine them carefully enough before joining – because, after all, you should be looking at what your agent can do for *you*, not only the other way around.

It put her in an impossible situation because they tried to demand she remain "exclusive" to their agency, but when you only get your artist one job a year… how is she meant to survive on that? She's a mum of two and had bills to pay so obviously she had to line up her own jobs on the side, and eventually she left the agency because they never did anything for her.

Another friend joined with a MAJOR London agency – think of the biggest one you can. We were all thrilled for her, but she actually lost a lot of her regular clients because they could no longer afford her; her agency was charging extortionate fees for simple jobs she otherwise would've been happy to do rather than sit at home doing nothing and earning no money. But for this agency, it was all about keeping up the appearance of exclusivity.

She remained with them for a little over a year and the next time I saw her after she left to go back to being freelance, she'd lost so much weight and was miserable. She told me that she "felt like a robot"; they would just send her off to jobs one after the other, never asking her what direction she'd like to take her career in or anything. She was just a money making machine to them and they didn't care personally about her at all. Of course, no one from the outside knew that she was miserable; they just looked on in awe that she was with this amazing agency.

I don't mean to be Debbie Downer and of course not everyone's experience will be like these but my point is: do some thorough research about what agencies you feel you'd personally fit in well with (both in terms of your style, their management style, and their client list). Don't just sign with the first one who shows you interest. You have nothing to lose by taking your time, maybe arranging a few meetings and seeing how you feel at the end.

Agent Meetings

If you finally land a meeting with the agent of your dreams, congratulations! And don't panic. I know it's so easy to spend time over thinking how the meeting will go, what you should wear, what images you should delete from your portfolio… Cast all of these worries out of your mind and just treat it like you're meeting a friend for coffee and getting to chat about your favourite subject: makeup! Dress how you usually would so you feel comfortable in the meeting and try not to stress too much about how the agent will perceive you; people never focus on us/our flaws anywhere near as much as we think they do, and either way you have no control over how they'll react to you. So just take a deep breath – you got this.

Make sure to bring your portfolio - this sounds like a given but my current agent, a week before she met with me, had met with another artist who "didn't realise" she needed to bring her book. Oops! Needless to say, this artist unfortunately did not get signed.

Name drop like your life depends on it; let them know all the photographers you work with, which clients you shot the campaigns for, which regular clients you shoot with, and so on. This will let them know you're both well connected within the industry and can bring money into the agency.

Finally, if there is anything you're not sure about – ask them! It's just like a "traditional" job interview where you should come prepared with some questions to ask them, too. This is to not only show your interest and knowledge of their agency, but to discover if they're the right fit for you.

Getting Jobs

If you do get signed to an agency, your career will now change. Any enquiries you now get personally should be forwarded to your agent (unless you've been given the OK to do your own jobs on the side, which is rare). You likely won't need to bother with invoices; your agent will simply send you a "Purchase Order (PO)" once they receive payment for a completed job and will transfer you the funds, minus the agency's cut.

Another word of warning here – agencies can be awful about paying you in a timely fashion! Some agencies are great and pay you as soon as they get paid but they are few and far between. It's been my experience (and really, just ask any model who's with an agency too) that most agencies like to hold off paying you for months, even if they received payment from the client long ago. This is usually because they like being able to collect interest on the amount for as long as possible, before transferring it to you. It's sneaky, it's annoying and I wish it wasn't like this, but it's just the nature of the business unfortunately. So if you were used to getting a certain amount (roughly) paid at the end of each month, say bye-bye to this security – you'll never know when you'll have invoices coming in. A part of joining an agency is giving away a huge part of control (something I personally really struggled with and still do to this day).

But otherwise, booking jobs will look the same as when you were handling bookings yourself. Instead, it'll just be your agent forwarding you on call sheets and references/moodboards, rather than the client directly. This part is actually a huge advantage; it weeds out all the fussy clients you used to have to deal with who would email you at all hours of the night with inane questions, expecting you to answer ASAP, or sending you millions of email chains while they prep for the shoot (and expect your input to each and every one). Instead, your lovely agent fields all the crazies for you! It's great.

In conclusion, like anything in life, there are pros and cons of joining an agency. But if you feel you'd like to take that next step and are ready to let someone else manage your career, it can be an incredibly exciting and rewarding time. For me, a week after I'd joined my first agency, I was sent to a mountaintop in Switzerland to shoot for US Vogue – something I very likely could never have accomplished by myself. Yes, you are handing over a percentage of your earnings, but look at it as though that money is going towards paying for a fantastic service not accessible by everyone. For me, it's worth it.

Final Word

Thank you so much for taking the time to read my book; I hope you learned some useful new tools to bring you all the success you desire as a makeup artist. We are lucky to live in a digital age where you can really take control of your own career path working as your own boss, and I hope this guide gave you a little more direction and inspiration on ways to achieve that.

The most important thing about being an artist, and what I hope you will take away from this book, is to never stop learning – not just technical skills as an artist but how to expand and maintain your business. There are enough mediocre makeup artists in the world… don't be another one.

Finally, please feel free to leave me a review to let me know how you got on with this book or if you think I've left anything important out. I'm always open to constructive criticism and improvement.

From one artist to another… good luck out there!

About the Author

Frida Bell is the pseudonym of a makeup artist based in London, U.K., but working internationally. Frida works primarily within the fashion (editorial and commercial) industry with big name clients like Ted Baker, Sony, Virgin, TK Maxx, John Lewis, HSBC, and many top fashion publications such as Marie Claire, Hunger, Wonderland, and Vogue.